LEAD FROM DAY ONE

A New Teacher's Guide to Becoming the Leader Their Students Deserve

RYAN MCHALE

Copyright © 2019 by Ryan McHale

All rights reserved.

No part of this book may be reproduced in any form or by any electronic or mechanical means, including information storage and retrieval systems, without written permission from the author, except for the use of brief quotations in a book review.

Published by EduMatch®
PO Box 150324, Alexandria, VA 22315
www.edumatch.org

All rights reserved. No portion of this book may be reproduced in any form without permission from the publisher, except as permitted by U.S. copyright law. For permissions contact sarah@edumatch.org.

These books are available at special discounts when purchased in quantities of 10 or more for use as premiums, promotions fundraising, and educational use. For inquiries and details, contact the publisher: sarah@edumatch.org.

ISBN: 978-1-970133-28-8

CONTENTS

Introduction   v
Preface   ix

Part One
SECTION ONE

1. Learn Your Community   3
2. Learn Your District   8
3. Learn from Your Mentor   12
4. The Power of Continuous Learning   18

Part Two
SECTION TWO

5. Get to Know Your Peers   25
6. Building Student Relationships   31
7. Family Engagement   35
8. Let Your Voice Be Heard   47

Part Three
SECTION THREE

9. Avoid the Perpetuation of Racial Inequities   55
10. Avoid an Overreliance on Platitudes   70
11. Avoid Taking Personally…   73
12. Avoid Falling into the Trap of Extreme Negativity   81
13. Avoid Neglecting Your Self-Care   84

Part Four
SECTION FOUR

14. Deliver High-Quality Instruction   93
15. Deliver Meaningful Feedback   100
16. Deliver Consistent Classroom Management   108
17. Deliver Continuous Social-Emotional Support   116
18. Deliver on Promises   124

19. Exit Ticket	130
References	133
About the Author	141
LEAD from Day One	143
Other EduMatch Titles	151
Notes	163

INTRODUCTION

Truth be told, teaching was not my first career choice. Back in the early 2000s as a young college student in Boston, I set out to be, of all things, a politician. Yes, you read that correctly. When I decided to attend Suffolk University, a medium-sized institution in the heart of Beantown, I had my heart set on going into politics. The idea of teaching the youth of America was nowhere to be found floating among the ADD-induced thoughts that continuously ran through my mind. And yet…here I am, writing a book aimed at motivating teachers, both new and seasoned. How did I get here? I guess you could say the writing was on the wall for many years. It just took me a while to see it. Nevertheless, when I did, I embarked on the greatest professional journey I could've ever imagined.

Teaching is a calling. It's a Jedi-like force that pushes us through the doors of our classrooms day in and day out. Regardless of the problems in education (and there are many), we return to our desks prior to the ringing of the morning bell because we know, in our hearts, that what we do can and will make a difference in our world. Teaching remains the profession most often joked about (and hated upon) by all those blinded by the irrational assumption that teachers are overpaid, lazy, and selfish. The truth? Teachers make the world go round. We provide the youth of our country with the academic and social enrichment that they'll need to thrive in a rapidly evolving society. Whether they care to admit it or not, those who criticize educators were at some point irrevocably mentored by someone in the very same position they now attempt to delegitimize.

With all the noise surrounding our profession, it can be hard to stay motivated. At some point in all of our careers, we will have that moment in which we question our purpose. We will ask ourselves if this job is worth it. We will ponder the impact we're actually having on our students. We will debate the merits of the job.

You'll eventually find yourself asking one monumental question — one that'll shape the rest of your life.

Is teaching worth it?

As I sit here reflecting upon my time as a classroom teacher, I can say, without the slightest of hesitations, that teaching is the most satisfying career imaginable. I mean, sure, would I have been disappointed to be as immensely inspirational as Barack Obama or as devilishly handsome as, say, Johnny Depp? Of course not. However, I'm not those men. I'll never be those men.

I am who I am. I'm Ryan McHale.

I'm an educator.

As are you.

Together, we're shaping the world.

So when you're sitting in your classroom after an unbelievably tough day, door closed, lights dimmed, tears cascading down your cheeks, remember that you're here for a reason. You're an educator because you believe in children. ALL children. It's not an easy job, but it's the one that called on you because the universe knew you could positively influence the amazing kids attending your school.

It's also important to note that your first years of teaching are incredibly challenging, and you'll undoubtedly be overwhelmed at various points within a given school year. Please understand that I've been there. I know how tough it can be. I am, in no way, asking or expecting any new or experienced teachers to take on every step outlined within the confines of this book. That would be asinine, to say the least. I would be complicit in the ever-rising numbers of educators leaving the profession due to burnout. The ultimate goal of *LEAD from Day One* is to outline a plan toward becoming a teacher leader. Implement suggestions as you see fit and as time allows. Move past that ideas that are simply not applicable due to the current needs of your students, school, and you. Create a timeline for the future implementation of suggestions. Take it slow while continually moving forward in your journey.

It takes a strong person to do this job. You have to be a leader. If you don't consider yourself an educational leader, it's time to start doing so right now. Whether you're a veteran teacher or you're in the midst of your first-year running the show, you can lead from the very first day of school. The purpose of this book is to help you see just how easily you can transform your entire mindset to become the leader your students need you to be. So forget about simply surviving the school year. It's time to believe that you'll find yourself thriving in the classroom.

You deserve it…

…And so do your students.

PREFACE

It's critically important to start by saying that anyone working within the confines of a school can be a leader. It doesn't matter if you're a baby-faced, brand new educator fresh out of college or a seasoned veteran who's only a couple of years away from a well-deserved siesta on a gorgeous beach far from the nearest classroom.

My journey to the classroom was unconventional. Within a matter of years, I went from wandering the halls of the Massachusetts State House to hiding within the confines of a small cubicle in Boston, and finally navigating my way through hallways jam-packed with over-stimulated pre-teens at a local middle school.

As I think back to all the events that led to writing a book on teaching, I can't help but recall (and appreciate) just how close my journey into the field of education came to ending before it had an opportunity to take off.

THE MOMENT WE'LL NEVER FORGET

For many adults, the moment they finally landed their first job — or at least the first job they *wanted* — is often a memory that fades over time. For educators? We will never forget the precise moment an administrator once told us, "Congratulations! You're the person we believe will positively impact the lives of countless students for years to come." Quite frankly, it's a split-second that'll stick with us until the day our personal dismissal bell rings for the final time.

I vividly remember the day I was offered my first official classroom teaching position. In was a sun-filled summer day in June 2010. At the time, I was working as a long-term substitute at a rather large middle school in Central Massachusetts. Despite my best efforts, I had been unable to secure a full-time position for the next year. Things looked bleak. I had no backup plan. I had fallen in love with education. Now an overwhelming amount of anxiety began to make attempts to relax (or sleep) seemingly futile. I had my fair share of interviews, and I thought I did well in all of them. But the phone never rang.

On the last day of my long-term substitute assignment, I walked out the door tightly grasping both ends of a W.B. Mason box filled with my personal effects. I was devastated to think my teaching career had just ended before it had the opportunity to truly begin. The seven months I had spent as a building substitute had filled my heart with such joy. It lit a fire within me. My passion set its sights on the field of education. There was no turning back now. Something had to give. Unfortunately, I was down to just one last chance to land a full-time teaching job for the 2010-2011 school year.

SO YOU'RE SAYING THERE'S A CHANCE...

The offer was for a 6th grade English language arts position about 25 minutes away from where my wife and I were living. I, without hesitation, accepted the offer to the delight of my family and friends. I had been working tirelessly to obtain a full-time position for months, and to be offered a job on the last day I was scheduled to work as a building substitute was simply astonishing.

As I drove home, I recall cruising down a scenic road, blaring some Phish jams, and finding it impossible to suppress the smile that left my cheekbones sore.

And then?

PREFACE

Well, a wave of terror swept through me at once.

Can I really do this?

Do I know anything about this town?

Do I have what it takes to reach my students and positively impact their lives, both academically and socially?

How can I provide my students with all that they need to find success inside and outside the classroom?

At that moment, I knew that the only way I could provide my soon-to-be students with the educational experience they deserve, I'd have to understand the inner workings of their town, the school district, and my assigned building. With less than two months until the first day of school, I had a lot to learn. I'm guessing it's the same way you're feeling right now.

Those feelings of panic, and trust me, they're legitimate, are probably racing through your mind at this point as well. Just breathe. You're going to be just fine. Regardless of whether you're a preservice teacher, a first-year educator, or still working your way toward tenure, you can be the educator your students deserve. Right now! Don't sit back and wait until you think you can finally take risks as a classroom teacher. Think of the hundreds of children that will come and go without getting your very best. Tentativeness will help no one. Be bold. Be a disruptor. Give each and every student that walks into your room the educational experience they deserve.

How will you do that? That's what I hope you'll get from this book. I hope to provide you with thought-provoking ideas, opportunities for self-reflection, and a plan of action to help you be the best educator for your kids. Do I have all the answers? Absolutely not, and I'll never claim to know it all. Instead, I hope to provide you with anecdotal evidence to support my thought process as an educator and point you in the direction of amazing leaders in the field. As I say to all my eighth-grade students I collaborate with each year, I'm not looking to indoctrinate. I'm hoping to share my experiences, amplify the voices of those who have additional expertise, and help you synthesize all that aforementioned information to shape your teaching practice. Once you're able to put it all together, you'll gain a level of self-confidence that'll transform your classroom into a safe and welcoming environment for all students — affording those children an opportunity to achieve a high level of academic and social growth under your mentorship.

BUT WAIT...WHAT DOES IT MEAN TO LEAD?

Before we prepare to jump into this journey together, now is a great time to delve into what teacher leadership truly means. Levenson (2014) notes that teacher leaders are instrumental not only from an instructional standpoint, but also from an institution and education policy perspective as well. Teacher leaders can operate in a formal or informal role (i.e., an additional stipend for completing leadership tasks) and "welcome knowledgeable supervision and support that would help them improve their practice" (Levenson, 2014, p.1). Before we move forward, let's take a moment to unpack Levenson's (2014) three pillars of successful teacher leadership):

- Instructional
- Institutional
- Education Policy

As we begin to understand the characteristics of a successful teacher leader, it's also critical to note that school administrators are central in creating a climate and culture that are conducive to triumphantly establishing an environment in which teacher leaders can thrive. It's certainly no easy task. So what are pivotal steps needed to be completed by administrators in order to help teacher leadership flourish? Dr. Jill Harrison Berg (2018), author of *Leading in Sync: Teacher Leaders and Principals Working Together for Student Learning*, outlined eight questions for administrators to consider when moving toward a teacher leadership model in an interview with TrustED:

1. Are regular conversations about teaching and learning happening in your building?
2. Do you have data that supports and focuses conversation about teaching and learning?
3. Do teachers feel as though they have permission to discuss data, teaching, and learning within each other's classrooms?
4. Do teachers know which colleagues they could approach with questions related to specific areas within the profession? For example, who is considered a resident expert in classroom management?
5. How do teachers in the building get questions surrounding teaching and learning answered quickly?
6. Are teachers within the building informed of what the latest education research is saying regarding best practices?
7. How are teachers engaging with family and community members for informational conversations related to teaching and learning?
8. Do teachers feel psychologically safe to take the risks that are necessary for bringing about improvements to the school community?

Dr. Berg's thought-provoking line of questioning directed toward administrators is something that we should all keep in the back of our minds as we consider moving into a teacher leadership role within our building. Do we feel as though our school's environment would allow us to comfortably pursue a leadership role? If not, I would humbly suggest that we consider approaching the administrative team, with Dr. Berg's questions in mind or hand, and discuss how teachers and administrators could work collaboratively to create a climate that's conducive to growing teacher leaders.

IT'S TIME TO GET TO WORK!

Now that we've been able to sort out what a teacher leader is and how your building administrator should be an accomplice in your efforts to bring about a culture of teacher leadership, it's time to get to work.

- It's time to immerse yourself in learning.
- It's time to engage stakeholders.
- It's time to avoid common pitfalls of teaching.
- It's time to deliver upon the responsibilities of today's classroom teacher.

Are you ready? Let's dive in with the first pillar of LEADing from day one: continuous learning.

SECTION ONE

Learn

LEARN YOUR COMMUNITY

I spent the months leading into my first year of teaching learning everything I could about the town I was preparing to serve. I knew I had to become familiar with so many different aspects of my newly acquired job in education. To be a successful first-year teacher, one must be willing to delve into the role — head-first, heart full — with a steadfast determination to take risks necessary to improve the lives of the students coming your way.

When I was hired to teach sixth-grade English language arts back in 2010, I knew very little about the community I was about to serve. Before my first interview, the only thing that I was able to recall about the town was that it was home to the 24-hour Wendy's off Interstate 495 that I frequented on my journey home following a concert at the local amphitheater. I had done enough research on student demographics, test scores, etc. to get through the interview process, but I knew I had only scratched the surface. If I were going to meet my students where they were in life, I knew I had to do better. I had to be better.

Understanding the ins and outs of the community in which you'll be serving is a critical aspect of successful teaching. Without a firm grasp of the surrounding area, educators will find it nearly impossible to empathize with the trials and tribulations that their students may encounter daily. Luckily, many districts are attempting to aid in the process of obtaining familiarity with the landscape of the neighborhood. Of the many options at a district's disposal, I've found the community bus tour to be most effective.

THE EYE-OPENING BUS TOUR

I had been quite anxious as my start date quickly approached. About four weeks from the first contractually obligated day of work for new hires, I received a packet in the mail that outlined the first two days of new teacher orientation. There was one part in particular that caught my eye.

As part of the mentoring program provided by my employer, I was to be afforded the opportunity to take a guided bus tour of the community. The tour guide? The superintendent. I was pleasantly surprised! After all, who better to inform new hires of the ins and outs of the community than the district leader? Knowing that I needed to quickly become acquainted with the town in which I'd soon be teaching, I saw this bus trip as a perfect first step. Suddenly, I felt the anxiety subside and the excitement grow.

Vivid memories of my first year teaching continue to take up a great deal of real estate in my mind — the bus tour as part of the new hire orientation being no exception. I remember standing off to the side of the road, along with over a dozen new educators, waiting for the bus to arrive. None of us spoke. I think we were all still a bit shook that our first day of teaching was a mere four days away. The silence, in those brief few moments, was deafening. It's funny thinking back to that moment now. The vast majority of us remain employed by the district. Hell, most of us have come to be great friends.

The apprehensiveness displayed from us that day is far from atypical. Frankly, it's a prime example of how overwhelming nerves tend to be as they rattle around the overwhelmed brains of all new teachers prior to the hallways of their building being flooded, wall-to-wall, with students. Suddenly, the dazed and confused new group of teachers were jolted out of their mid-morning reverie by the arrival of a run-of-the-mill, yellow school bus.

As helpful as I found the new hire bus trip to be, it's vital that the experience is done right. The neighborhood tour could either be a monumental success with the journey truly resonating with those in attendance or it can be yet another well-intentioned, yet poorly executed, aspect of education. For the tour to positively impact the lives of those involved, the following three components should be discussed and implemented within the activity:

1. Community Involvement

While it's terrific to have the superintendent leading the tour throughout the neighborhood, the fact of the matter is that they may not live in the town or city. They will surely know most of the surface-level information as it relates to the district. But is that enough? It shouldn't be. We should yearn to know what's below the surface. What makes the community tick? To get that information requires first-hand knowledge. A successful guided tour should include a variety of local citizens. Perhaps the tour can stop at several different spots around town, and a guest can jump aboard for a few moments to give you their perspectives on the area.

Who would make for good guests? I would recommend having a parent/guardian or student from each part of town come aboard to share their story. It'll provide you with an opportunity to see that not all areas of the same town/city are created equal. Such a distinction will become vital as you develop plans to differentiate your instructional practices throughout the school year.

I'd also highly recommend having a member of the school committee, a local politician, as well as local business owners say a few words to all those on the tour. Hearing different voices and experiences will allow you to obtain an accurate, up-to-date pulse on the area. As we'll discuss later, quickly building relationships with students will be of utmost importance, and there's no better way to help you do just that than by having a clear understanding of the place they call home.

. . .

2. Conspicuous Travel

While the intent of a neighborhood tour is undoubtedly done in good faith, the impact of the event can be devastating to students and families if planned without regard to the feelings of those living in the area. The bus trip is not a Hollywood Trolley Tour. You should not have your phones out taking pictures or videos. The tour is not for entertainment purposes.

I remember discussing on Twitter the need for districts to offer such tours to new hires at the start of each school year. I remember a young woman commenting on my tweet, and I'll never forget her comments. She went on to tell me that she grew up in the poorest part of her town, in the roughest of apartment complexes, with trash scattered throughout the main entrance. She said that walking to her apartment reminded her of a post-apocalyptic film.

I immediately felt a strong surge of empathy rush through my body. She did not wish to start an argument right then and there, but she did desire to point out that she would have been mortified to walk out of her apartment to see a school bus full of teachers staring at her, cameras in head, and whispering what she would only assume to be remarks of negativity to their neighbor. She was right.

Conducting a neighborhood tour should not be a show. It should not be a time for the adults to get on and off the bus to conduct investigations. It should not be a time to gossip.

The tour should be a time to watch and listen. Soak in everything you can and spend time processing what you learned!

3. Time to Unpack and Discuss

One of the most important parts to successful professional development is being afforded the opportunity to reflect on what you've learned and discuss your takeaways and lingering questions with colleagues. When it comes to the aforementioned neighborhood tour, such collaboration is critical. You've just had an eye-opening last few hours learning the ins and outs of the area. You are also undoubtedly realizing that most of what you saw will have an impact on the children who'll be outside your door on day one. It's ok to be nervous at this point. Take the time to unpack and discuss.

After my tour of the neighborhood during the first day of orientation, I remember sitting around a cafeteria table with my principal and six other new hires. We talked at great length — not only about what we noticed, but HOW those observations would impact our job.

One's ability to build powerful relationships with students is THE key to being a successful educator. There's no other way around it.

The most sure-fire way of gaining a child's trust to build that bond? Learning all you can about who they are and where they're coming from! As original Freedom Writer, Manny Scott, said of today's youth during his powerful keynote address at ASCD's Empower18 Conference in Boston, Massachusetts, "They can learn. They are just waiting for you to meet them on their level (Scott, 2018)."

LEARN YOUR DISTRICT

In public education, all decisions should be subjected to checks and balances from stakeholders. And when it comes to education, there are a lot of stakeholders: administrators, teachers, students, parents and guardians, school committee members, community leaders, and others. For a school district to provide each child with the educational journey they are entitled to by the 14th Amendment to the United States Constitution (U.S. Const. amend. XIV), stakeholders must work collaboratively to ensure that today's students are allowed to thrive, both academically and socially.

As a new teacher, joining a new district's team is a massive responsibility. You're tasked with getting up to speed with a district's mission to seamlessly transition in a way that will allow students to demonstrate growth in a manner the district has deemed most appropriate. Once hired, I always recommend new teachers do the following:

1. Review the district's mission statement
2. Examine the district's long-term improvement plan
3. Analyze student demographics

In completing the three aforementioned tasks, you will set not only yourself, but most importantly, your students up for success once the new school year officially begins. Let's delve deeper into each of the three actionable items.

REVIEW DISTRICT MISSION STATEMENT

The good news is that you've probably started doing your homework in this area in preparation for your initial interview. If so, great! If not, now's a great time to head over to your district's website and review all materials related to its mission statement. Such materials may also include a strategic plan that is designed to help ensure the district, as a whole, is progressing toward, meeting, or exceeding the goals outlined in the mission statement. What a district writes within its mission statement says a lot about its dedication to helping all children thrive.

A district's mission statement should serve as a guiding light to stakeholders as they work on updating policies, curricula, and other documents. It's their beacon of truth. It defines the district to its very core. When I examine a district's mission statement, I'm looking for signs of inclusivity, student safety (both physically and mentally), a commitment to both academic rigor and social-emotional learning, and a willingness to provide teachers with what they need to ensure each child succeeds.

So what does your district's mission statement say? How will you work to uphold those standards as you jump into your new position?

EXAMINE THE DISTRICT'S LONG-TERM IMPROVEMENT PLAN

While a well-written mission statement helps us understand what a school currently expects from stakeholders within the building, the district's long-term improvement plan is just as vital to planning your school year. Where is the district hoping to go in the coming years? Will those target objectives ultimately affect how you build lesson plans? It may prove helpful to start moving in the direction of future goals now. For example, if you know that your district will soon go to a 1:1 setting, it makes sense to begin writing units that incorporate the upcoming increase in educational technology.

Likewise, if the district is outlining a soon-to-be-implemented text selection tool, it makes sense to begin analyzing your curriculum's list of novels. Would those novels fit the new tool? If not, advocate to your mentor or building administrator for new texts. Are there novels that you feel would be a better fit? If so, bring them in now! It'll save you much frustration later when you're under pressure to overhaul academic resources.

ANALYZE STUDENT DEMOGRAPHICS

Just as it is essential to understand the community in which you serve, it's also critical to get a sense of WHO your students are before their arrival. One of the most anticipated days of my summer is finally receiving my class rosters for the upcoming school year. Yes, I know the summers are short, and my unabashed excitement sounds completely geeky. However, time is of the essence!

When I get my class rosters, I'm on the prowl for a couple of things in particular. I'll be looking at Special Education Status, EL or FLEP status, as well as past grades in my content area. It's crucial to understand the education history of students if we're, as Manny Scott (2018) said, to meet students where they are. What modifications or accommodations are recommended to assist students in the classroom? Such information will allow you to plan for differentiation down the line.

The one thing that I did not examine? The disciplinary history of students. As a new teacher, you may be "warned" of students who have, in the past, engaged in what is perceived by some as problematic behavior. If you're a returning educator, I'm sure you'll know of the "reputation" of certain students by merely seeing their name on your roster. We must remember that kids deserve a fresh start each school year. If I were to look closely at a student's disciplinary record, I'm likely to go into the school year with preconceived notions about that child. As educators, we must avoid this practice at all costs.

We need to be at the classroom door on day one wide-eyed and smiling at every single student. We must make sure all kids feel safe and welcomed in our presence, in our room, and in our building. Can we do that if we've already decided that a child is a so-called, "heavy-hitter?" Our assumptions are based on past events. Leave them in the past. Focus on the child's present and future. Let them know that it's not about what they may have done in the past. It's not about what other teachers may have thought about them in the past. Let them know that you're here, you care, and that this year will be a stepping stone leading to a future filled with endless possibilities.

LEARN FROM YOUR MENTOR

Without question, one of the most influential people in your life at the start of your career will be your school-assigned mentor. In most cases, your mentor — often assigned by the building leadership team — will be a member of your content-specific department. As such, your mentor will be able to assist in you becoming acclimated with curriculum, pacing guides, grading policies, and more. I can't stress enough just how vital this person should be during the beginning stages of your career.

I loved my mentor. She was one of the most respected ELA educators in the building and a wonderful human being. However, I look back and wished I had leaned on her more while in my formative years in teaching. Perhaps it was ego. Perhaps I thought I would figure it out on my own. Whatever the reason, I failed to take advantage of a great teacher's offering of support and guidance. While I made it through my first years without incident, I didn't thrive in the classroom. I survived. When it comes to teacher efficacy, there's a stark difference between thriving and surviving in the classroom. Survival doesn't typically lend itself to providing students with an equitable opportunity to master the curriculum.

If you're thriving in the classroom, you're confident. You're approachable. You are continually learning. Student voices are amplified, and the classroom is alive! Learning and collaboration are noticeable the moment someone walks in the door. Students are engaged, and you're in the groove -- providing direct instruction, giving real-time feedback, and attending to the social-emotional needs of every child.

In contrast, you'll know pretty quickly when you've morphed into an educator in survival mode. That vibrant classroom? Gone. Instead, you walk through the door and immediately feel as though you're on Willy Wonka's psychedelic boat ride (Margulies, Wolper, & Stuart, 1971). The initial fire in your belly? It's slowly burning out. Anxiety and panic start to creep into your mind.

> *Not a speck of light is showing*
> *So the danger must be growing*
> *Are the fires of Hell a-glowing*
> *Is the grisly reaper mowing?*
> *Yes, the danger must be growing*
> *For the rowers keep on rowing*
> *And they're certainly not showing*
> *Any signs that they are slowing!*
> *(Dahl, 2005)*

Sure, perhaps I'm a bit melodramatic here, but the truth remains the same. Your first years of teaching are a whirlwind. It's a roller-coaster. Some days you'll leave knowing you did your part to help make dozens and dozens of children better in some small way. Other days you'll be left drowning in tears wondering if it's too late to make a career change. It's normal. And it's ok.

Your mentor will be there. Waiting. They will know what you're going through because they've been there before. Do not let your pride get in the way of thriving during your first years of teaching. Allow yourself to be vulnerable and share your experiences, your fears, and more with your mentor. A great mentor can positively impact your career in ways you've never imagined...but only if you let them.

I still wish I had.

HOW TO MAKE THE MOST OF THE MENTOR-MENTEE RELATIONSHIP

As I've said, my mentor was and continues to be one of the most respected educators in the district. She works tirelessly to balance the need for rigorous teaching with building strong relationships to ensure the social-emotional well-being of her students. It's a balance that I'm continually reflecting upon and trying to improve. I know I'll get there eventually, but the truth remains the same: I would have figured it out sooner had I fully made the most of my mentor's willingness to help.

So, after years of pondering the significance of the mentor-mentee relationship in education, I've come to realize that there are ways to help create and sustain a mutually-beneficial partnership that will allow for both parties to grow as stronger classroom teachers.

1. Focus on Building Relationship

It's certainly understandable to be nervous heading into your first meeting with your mentor. After all, this new peer will be your lifeline throughout the start of your career. You'll feel as though your relationship with this person must be perfect. But please remember... perfection is not reality. That said, a healthy relationship will make for a smooth transition into your new role as a classroom teacher.

When you first meet with your mentor, I'd encourage you to not focus on the day-to-day tasks and overall curricula conversations. Such conversations are a must and will happen down the line. But on day one? The main objective should be to get to know one another — not just as educators, but as human beings.

Consider grabbing lunch together outside the building. Spend time conversing about each other's background, family, and general interests. Trust me: as an introvert, the idea of small talk with a new acquaintance sounds like a nightmare. However, building a strong rapport with your mentor will help lay down the foundation upon which your new career will be built.

. . .

2. Develop Short-Term and Long-Term Goals

Goal setting is a frequently-heard phrase in education. Whether you are setting goals for yourself or your students, goals are everywhere you turn, as they should be. Establishing goals allows us to chart a path toward success.

You will also want to create and seek successful completion of predetermined goals set by you and your mentor. You'll certainly want to set lofty end-of-year goals. That's a given. However, I'd also suggest considering adding many short-term goals that'll build upon one another and help ensure that you ultimately meet that long-term goal. For example, if one of your primary goals is to create a classroom environment that is conducive to amplifying the voices of all students, be sure to check in consistently throughout the year. Make adjustments when necessary.

3. Mutual Respect

For the mentor-mentee relationship to be truly effective, there must be mutual respect between both parties. As you get to know one another, you may notice subtle differences in educational philosophy, classroom management preferences, etc. I don't believe that small differences in viewpoint are a deal-breaker for the partnership. However, there will need to be mutual respect. At the end of the day, you'll both be working tirelessly to bring about an equitable educational experience to children. There may be slight differences in delivery methods, but I believe that so long as the mission is the same, then mutual respect will lead to a successful mentorship pairing.

4. Trust

As long as there is mutual respect between the mentor and mentee, both parties should find it easy to trust one another. Trust is a critical component of any mentoring program. While a mentor will certainly observe you in the classroom setting over the school year, such observations should be conducted informally and not be a part of your summative review. As a result, you should find yourself willing and able to discuss your performance without fearing that your comments and the feedback ascertained from your observation will be relayed to the administrative team.

5. Value Feedback

There is only one true way for mentorship to be particularly useful. There must be the free exchange of feedback with suggested, actionable steps given as a means to improve practice. Getting feedback as a new educator will never be easy. We all want to believe that we will hit the ground running as a fully capable educator with all the tools needed for success at your disposal. The truth is that we don't get it right the first time. Frankly, I'm still working on getting everything right ten years into this roller coaster ride.

I'd offer that the key to growing as an educator is to value feedback and lean into what your mentor is saying. Don't get defensive. Actively listen. Reflect on what is being said. Does your mentor have a valid point? Is it something that should be improved upon? Or do you believe there may have been a misunderstanding? Is there something you'd like to clarify? In any event, feedback given is an opportunity for both parties to engage in helpful dialogue that'll eventually assist in all parties involved becoming better educators.

BUT WHAT IF THINGS AREN'T WORKING OUT?

It would be wonderful if schools were able to get mentor-mentee pairings right the first time. And, for the most part, many buildings do a nice job matching a new teacher with a veteran educator who matches up well with the rookie. However, sometimes building administrators, for a litany of reasons, get it wrong. It's just the nature of having to predict how two adult professionals will mesh in a collaborative setting. That doesn't mean you have to accept being a part of a mentorship that is negatively impacting how you view your new job, or attempts to rain down upon the burning fire that's currently flowing through your body like lava traveling down the sides of a ruptured volcano.

We've discussed the need to build a strong relationship with your mentor. Without a solid bond, it's going to be extremely challenging to speak your truths in a manner that will allow both parties to grow as educators. An inability to talk openly and honestly with one another will make for future mentor-mentee meetings a waste of time. You'll both be going through the motions, and there will be little to no growth in your development. If you do not feel as though your current partnership is helping you become the teacher you've always wanted to be, do not be afraid to air your concerns with your administrative team.

While it can be distressing to relay your concerns to your principal so early in your career, understand that it is part of their job to ensure you are placed in a position to succeed. You (and your incoming students) deserve nothing less. If you express your concerns about your mentorship in a manner that suggests the stated objectives of the building's mentoring program are not being met, it behooves your administrator to both work with you and your mentor to ensure future success or place you with a colleague who can help meet your needs as a new teacher. Of course, if going straight to administration seems overly daunting, consider speaking with your Professional Learning Network (PLN), which we'll be discussing a bit later! Regardless of the route you choose, never hesitate to express concerns regarding a failing mentorship. The effective mentoring of a new teacher is critical in bucking the trend of educators leaving the profession far too soon.

THE POWER OF CONTINUOUS LEARNING

As educators, one of our primary objectives should be to help transform our young students into lifelong learners. One of the easiest ways to assist the kids in changing their mindset regarding education is to model what it looks like to be a lifelong learner. Show them that learning should never stop. Help them see the benefits of continuous learning!

For many of the young children swarming your classroom day in and day out, they see school as a compliance task. It's something that needs to be done. Nothing more. Nothing less. As we begin to understand what tasks will be necessary for children to find success in the workplace of the future, it's clear that school needs to be more than just a task. It needs to be an academic awakening. As a classroom leader, you have the opportunity to help students see the benefits of continually pushing the envelope, seeking answers to complex problems, and becoming scholars in every sense of the word.

However, we must remember that doing so will not be an easy task. It's difficult for young kids to simply take our word for...well...anything. They need concrete evidence to show that a continual thirst for knowledge will create a path of future success. We must strive to become the living embodiment of constant learning. The good news is that it's now easier than ever to grow as educators.

EXPLOSION OF #EDUTWITTER

Over the last few years, we have seen a growing number of educators flock to Twitter as a means of improving their own practice. Since all aspects of Twitter are currently free to all users, teachers have the innate ability to freely express their views on all things education while connecting with other educators, consultants, and experts from around the world. With tweets limited to just 280 characters, users are forced to write concise thoughts and link to further evidence to back up their views. "Tweeters" will then have the ability to leave comments in hopes of engaging in a healthy debate related to the topic at hand.

One of the greatest functions of Twitter is the ability to participate in group chats. The chats allow for a free-flowing stream of ideas during a set period. There are many education chats on Twitter these days. Quite frankly, it's hard to discern which ones are worth your participation. Before hightailing it to the first edu-chat you find, a period of self-reflection would be highly beneficial. What are you hoping to get out of a Twitter chat? Are you looking for a 30-minute quick-chat focused solely on the rainbows and sunshine of education as a means of sustaining positive vibes? Are you currently hoping to learn more about equity in education? Is Special Education an area of education in which you're hoping to become more proficient?

While all EDUchats have their merit (and are certainly worth future consideration), joining any and all chats you come across may not be as helpful as you'd think. Fully participating and growing as an educator through such chats require time, time you may not have early in your career. Be thoughtful and choose wisely. As you become more confident in your teaching practices, reach out to the leaders of particular chats to become a guest moderator, and help other educators grow.

With that said, if you're brand new to the #EduTwitter landscape, I highly recommend jumping on board with any/all of the following moderated chats:

#ClearTheAir #CelebratED #HipHopEd #EdChat
#EDUColor #DisruptTexts #MasteryChat #EquityinED

All of these aforementioned Twitter chats will push your thinking. While many online chats can be filled with over-the-top platitudes and pats on the back, these specific discussion groups will ask you to step outside your comfort zone. You'll be confronted with difficult questions. You'll make mistakes. You'll have to sit with those mistakes. But you'll learn. And you'll grow. That's what #EduTwitter SHOULD be all about.

WORD OF CAUTION

While Twitter certainly has helped in increasing professional development opportunities for educators across the globe, it is important to take time to vet information and data that is widely shared on the platform. In this era of fake news, it is easier than ever to promote incorrect information and have it spread like wildfire across the #EduTwitter landscape.

Educator and blogger Blake Harvard touched upon this very issue in a post titled, "Out of Cite, Out of Mind," on his website, The Effortful Educator (2018). In the blog entry, Harvard touches upon examples of data that is commonly shared across the internet without any mentioning of evidence. So, what's the harm in retweeting misleading or in some cases, patently false information, to your network? I'll let Mr. Harvard take it from here:

> *So, what's the big deal? Why does it matter that this image exists in edutwitterland? Because teachers retweet and unknowingly spread false information, influencing other impressionable teachers. Because teachers use this material as fact and adjust their instruction accordingly. Because teachers participate in professional development opportunities where this information is used and discussed. Because teachers deserve informed and*

evidence-based statistics when deciding how to run their classroom.

While Twitter has certainly changed the game as it relates to professional growth opportunities for teachers, it, like any other social media platform, certainly gives users reason to pause and reflect upon what's out there. It's important always to ask questions. Who is disseminating this information? Whose voice is being amplified through the tweet? Whose voice is being silenced? Why might this person want me to believe the data in front of me? Is this person trying to sell me on a product? All of these questions are more than valid and worth considering when perusing Twitter. Don't be afraid to ask the original poster for clarification! If they are recommending changing the way you lead your classroom, it's worth a full investigation to discern the merit of said comments.

NEVER. STOP. READING.

There was a time early in my career when I couldn't tell you the last book (professionally related or otherwise) that I had read. I'm full of anguish and shame as I think of all the amazing literature I could have been keeping up with, especially related to the field of education. It seems like there are always new EduBooks popping up left and right. Each new book comes promising the latest and greatest update to pedagogy and the like. While some books will be more beneficial and closely tied to your career path, it's the continuous desire to learn and grow through reading that'll eventually help make you a stronger educator.

Today, I never leave a bookstore without a new purchase. Whether it is a book on teaching or a new novel, poetry collection, or nonfiction text that I'll eventually introduce to my curriculum, I'm always on the hunt for new insight. Often you'll be recommended texts from your mentor, peers, online professional learning community, etc. Trust me when I say that you'll rarely be led to reading a text unworthy of your time and intellectual stimulation.

As I read, I always have a legal pad and pen somewhere near me. I love taking notes both inside the margins of books as well as on separate paper. As an adult continually fighting to push through the symptoms of Attention Deficit Disorder, I rely heavily on annotated notes. While ADD isn't always the easiest to overcome in this profession, it's certainly doable. The reason that I've been able to learn continuously over the years has been through the outside reading.

Set a personal reading goal this year! Take notes. Apply what you've learned either within your classroom or the outside world. You'll be glad you did!

Looking for recommendations to add to your collection? While certainly not a comprehensive list, here are some of my go-to books on education that can help you navigate through the first years in the profession:

- *Dare to Lead* by Brené Brown
- *The Teacher Wars* by Dana Goldstein
- *Even on Your Worst Day, You Can Be A Student's Best Hope* by Manuel Scott
- *Ghosts in the Schoolyard* by Eve. L. Ewing
- *This is Not a Test* by Jose Luis Vilson
- *Why Are All the Black Kids Sitting Together in the Cafeteria* by Dr. Beverly Daniel Tatum
- *Lies my Teacher Told Me* by James W. Loewen
- *Leadership* by Peter G. Northouse

A great teacher is one who is always learning — learning about their students and families, the community, the district and school, and, most importantly, themselves. It's a never-ending cycle of learning and growing. Failure to put time and effort into continuous learning can lead to burnout and, eventually, becoming an ineffective educator. Simply put, education is rapidly changing. As it evolves, so must we.

SECTION TWO
Engage

GET TO KNOW YOUR PEERS

As with any workplace environment, one of the most predictive measures, as it relates to overall job satisfaction, is your relationship with peers. While a school may be quite different from the run-of-the-mill office setting, it's true that how we get along with our fellow educators can go a long way in shaping us as teachers. Let's be honest for a second. If you're surrounded by negative educators (or at least unfriendly ones), you're far more likely to find yourself swirling down a black hole of negativity. As a result, that well filled with enormous enthusiasm for education that you've been oozing since your time as a pre-service teacher could end up running dry.

COLLABORATION IS KEY

The notion that teachers are notoriously isolated is not a new idea. However, research has shown that collaboration among educators is one of the best ways to help students grow, both academically and socially, within a given school year. A 2015 study published in the *American Educational Research Journal* found that higher levels of teacher collaboration had positive effects on both student achievement and teacher improvement (Ronfeldt, Farmer, McQueen, & Grissom, 2015). And it makes perfect sense. We are only better together.

I remember my first year in the classroom and the hesitation that I felt as it related to engaging in helpful work-related dialogue with peers. Looking back, I'm still unsure as to why I remained so quiet that first year. Perhaps I was just so eager to prove myself as a young (semi-young, I suppose) teacher. I wanted to show everyone that I was the right choice for the job. To be honest, I'm quite sure that chip on my shoulder was as a result of the initial interview process. I knew I hadn't performed as well as I could have during those meetings, and, as a result, there were several educators who weren't on board with my hiring. Thankfully, the principal of the building saw something in me. Saw the potential I possessed and gave me a shot. I'm still hopeful that she feels she made the right call ten years ago.

But I digress.

The chip that was firmly implanted on my right shoulder got in the way of meaningful moments of collaboration. I was stubborn. I thought I had the answers to the test from day one. While confidence plays a significant role in teacher efficacy, too much will impact you, your peers, and your students in a negative way. You can't lead from day one if you feel like you've mastered the profession from day one. As original Freedom Writer, Manny Scott, frequently cautions educators, "Stay Humble."

The best educators realize that we can do more for our students by working together with each other. It seems simple, yet, for a myriad of reasons, we struggle to engage in meaningful collaboration with our peers. So what steps can we take to help promote leaning on one another to improve our instructional practices? Aside from effectively utilizing contractual meeting time, there are a few out-of-the-box ideas that may help boost faculty members working in concert.

1. Create a PLC

The implementation of a Professional Learning Community, a group of educators working collaboratively to research and introduce new strategies in the area of instructional practice, classroom management, and more, has become quite the trend in education. And for good reason! With time seemingly always of the essence, it helps to have a team in place to assist in the bringing about of new ideas within the school setting.

With the installation of a PLC, teachers within a group can assign each other jobs and then come together to review all the information gathered. With everything literally on the table, your group can synthesize the data in front of you to help make an informed decision.

Noted education researcher John Hattie has frequently discussed the value of teachers working collaboratively to assist in helping students demonstrate academic growth. Hattie (2018) lists collective teacher efficacy[1] as the number one, school-led influence on student learning. While it would be optimal if each school across the nation were equipped to establish an environment that would allow teacher efficacy to thrive, we are unfortunately not yet at that point. However, we can work collaboratively with administrators to help create a sustainable culture that promotes efficacy.

According to a 2007 report authored by Dana Brinson and Lucy Steiner (The Center for Comprehensive School Reform and Improvement), school administrators can work to improve teacher efficacy through the completion of four tasks:

1. Help teachers build instructional knowledge and skills.
2. Create opportunities for educators to regularly meet to share out their skills and areas of expertise.
3. Interpret incoming data and, with a keen eye on transparency, provide actionable feedback to educators.
4. Get teachers involved in the decision-making process.

2. The Rise of the Book Club

Education books are all the rage these days *(wink)*! There are so many valuable resources out there yet so little time to peruse it all. As much as we'd love to read book after book regarding our field, the reality is that there isn't enough time to read it all ourselves. This is where the book club within your school can be of some assistance.

As you come across books that you genuinely feel could benefit the faculty, staff, and administration of your building, reach out to them. Suggest forming a book club with weekly meetings scheduled for after school. Perhaps you can even do low-key gatherings at a local restaurant or bookstore! As folks sign up, assign individuals certain parts of the book. Each member will then come to the meeting ready to discuss the critical points of their section. As such, you'll lessen the personal reading time required while still being introduced to the vital elements contained within the work.

There are hundreds of prospective books out there that would meet the needs of you and your colleagues. Among the terrific options available to you are:

- *Beyond Test Scores* by Jack Schneider
- *White Rage* by Dr. Carol Anderson
- *White Fragility* by Robin DiAngelo
- *So You Want to Talk About Race* by Ijeoma Oluo
- *Learning Transformed* by Tom Murray and Eric Sheninger
- *It's the Mission, Not the Mandates* by Dr. Amy Fast

3. Lunch Bunch

Now, I'm a big proponent of the silent lunch. I need those precious 30 minutes to recharge my batteries and mentally prepare for the day's final stretch. However, if you find yourself struggling to find time to collaborate with peers, starting a lunch group is always an option.

While a lunch bunch may seem like an unattractive option for collaborating with peers, you can certainly work to spice it up a bit. Consider having meetings every other Friday with each member of the group rotating to bring in a homemade meal. Alternatively, you can raffle off a gift (perhaps a book, markers, pencils, etc.) for those in attendance. The lunch bunch may not be the most exciting option when it comes to building a culture of collaboration, but it's certainly always something to have in your back pocket.

CLUSTERS OF CONSISTENCY FOR THE KIDS

In schools around the country, many elementary and middle schools operate within a team-based system. This format groups students into clusters with the kids rotating between the same handful of teachers. For example, I typically will have 110-125 students each year (divided into five English language arts classes). These same students will have also have the same Social Studies, Science, Math, and World Language teacher throughout the year. While this system certainly has its fair share of pros and cons, recent research has revealed that the cluster format leads to greater academic and social growth for students.

One of the better characteristics of the cluster format is the consistency that is afforded to the students due to this setup. As a team, my colleagues and I meet every two days per six-day scheduling cycle. Because we all share the same students, we can discuss student performance, share classroom management strategies, and plan team building activities for the kids.

The cluster format aids in bringing about a sense of community and consistency for our students. However, to be truly successful, the teachers on the team must be willing and able to trust one another, share resources, and be on the same page when it comes to the basics of academic and social expectations.

If your school does not currently operate within a cluster setting? Reach out to a handful of peers to create a PLC. Conduct yourselves as you would, had you been placed together in a cluster. Over time, you may find more and more colleagues desiring to follow your lead. What a fantastic display of leadership!

YOU'LL NEED A SUPPORT SYSTEM

Another hugely important reason to get to know your peers as soon as possible is the simple fact that you're going to need a support system throughout the year. The start of every school year is like hopping on to an intense roller-coaster of emotion. Undoubtedly, you'll experience the highest of highs during the year. However, do not let anyone fool you into thinking you'll go through the year unscathed. Sorry. It just isn't going to happen. And when those moments of doubt, anger, or sadness creep up and attempt to make you question your career decisions (Kidding…sort of!), you'll want and NEED someone to lean on.

When you have someone (or perhaps you formed your own squad!), you gain confidence in knowing that there exists a safe place for you within the confines of the school building. Whether you need to vent, cry, or just gather your thoughts for a few moments, your colleague will be there with open arms and an open door. They'll be there to accompany you on a quick walk to the corner store to grab some much-needed caffeine and sugar-filled snacks.

Come the following summer, as you're sitting on the beach reflecting on the past year, you'll remember all those times your squad had your back. How they selflessly put their needs on pause to help lift you. You'll remember how they saved you from vanquishing into a mindset of defeat and uncertainty. You'll want to call them right then and there to say how much you appreciate their friendship. But honestly? After all you've been through together? There's a good chance they'll already be sitting right next to you on the beach, passing you a cold drink, and preparing a toast for a job well done.

BUILDING STUDENT RELATIONSHIPS

Of all the things to accomplish in the early stages of the school year, working to build student relationships is at the very top of the list. From day one, we should be working tirelessly to make a sincere connection with the children we'll be collaborating with over the course of the school year. What kids truly want and need is to come into a building every day surrounded by adults who are truly invested in their academic and social growth.

Why do we place such tremendous emphasis on building healthy relationships with students right from the get-go? It's all about the learning. Over the years, I've seen that the students who have made the most significant academic gains within a given school year are the ones that felt comfortable in my classroom. It wasn't because I attempted to infuse humor at times or that I played music during class. It was more than that.

What mattered most to the students who found success in my class was that I created a classroom environment that was built upon mutual respect, trust, understanding, and accountability. With such an environment in place, students were comfortable and ready to engage in active learning. It all starts by setting the tone from day one.

SETTING THE RIGHT TONE

One of the clichés typically tossed around during the first days of school is "Set the tone!" I do not disagree with the statement in general. I disagree with the negative connotation associated with the comment. When we hear "Set the tone!" during the early stages of the year, we tend to hear something harsh. We tend to hear "Show them who's boss! You aren't their friend. Let them know that now!" I refuse to believe that's the most effective way to go about tone setting at the start of the school. Not by a longshot.

The first couple of days of school should focus very little on academics. The focus should be entirely on making connections and building trust. "Set the tone!" should refer to the need to make children feel comfortable with us and our classroom setting. It should be a phrase that promotes positivity and joy for the upcoming journey.

Despite what you may have learned during your pre-service career, it is more than possible to have a great relationship with students while simultaneously holding them accountable through rigorous expectations. That great relationship makes it easier to push kids past what they think they can even do because they trust you! They know why you're standing in front of them. It's not to push them around because of some inner desire for power. It's not to make them feel bad for their mistakes. It's to help them be the best human being they can be. You are there to light a fire in their belly. You are there to be another adult in their life who's doing their best to help them navigate through the craziness of today's society.

So, yes. Be sure to set the tone on that first day of school. Just be sure to set the right tone.

THE IMPORTANCE OF TRUST

Any dynamic relationship in this world requires trust among all parties. Without it, the sustainability of such a bond would be undeniably tricky. Consider the relationship between a teacher and student. The goal of the relationship is to assist the student in achieving academic and social growth while simultaneously allowing yourself to learn from the student (of their family, culture, hobbies, etc.). It's a delicate relationship and one that'll require both individuals to grant one another a high level of trust.

Regardless of your role within education, you are asking for the trust of all stakeholders to teach all students properly. As a classroom teacher, you are asking students and their families to trust that you are making decisions that are in the best interest of the child. Whether it concerns your homework policy or curricula choices, having their unwavering trust will give you the confidence to deliver an enriching educational experience to each student.

If you're an administrator, you're asking for the trust of your faculty and staff to make decisions that will ultimately promote student learning while simultaneously ensure they will not suffer from burnout as a result of the new endeavor.

If you're a special education teacher, you're relying on the trust of the classroom teacher to take control of differentiation, modifications, and accommodations if you feel the best interests of the child are not being met.

If you're a student, you're asking the educators in front of you to trust that they'll listen and be attentive to your needs as a scholar. You're asking that they will not wield their power as the adult in the room to demean you, unfairly issue consequences, and attempt to hold you back from thriving in this world.

Trust is a critical aspect of any healthy relationship. As the center of the edu-universe continues to discuss the importance of relationships and putting "Maslow before Bloom," putting a clear emphasis on trust will allow your working relationships with students to flourish.

THE POWER OF VULNERABILITY

When I think back to my own experiences in school, I often find myself recalling teachers that acted robotically. It's hard to remember attempts at a joke to lighten the mood or the sharing of an anecdote from their own lives to help us connect with a lesson. Instead, many of my teachers chose to remain void of any discernible emotion, preferring to "stick to the script." I can't help but wonder if that lack of sincere passion and a willingness to connect with the children in front of them made it challenging for me to buy-in to what they were selling.

I don't blame my former teachers for running their classrooms in that manner. It's more probable than not that they were instructed to act that way during their years of preparation for entering the field of education. And did it work for some kids? Absolutely. But it certainly didn't work for all. There remains talk that teachers should resist the desire to be vulnerable in front of their students. That it's somehow wrong to discuss our struggles, poor choices, and the things we wish we could do differently. That's an enormous problem.

Successful leadership, whether it's leading a classroom, a school, or a district, requires vulnerability. We've talked about the need to develop strong, healthy relationships with our students, but how can we do that if we are unwilling to make ourselves vulnerable? Students can spot a fake teacher from a mile away. They know when you genuinely care and when you're merely trying to check off a box found on a random classroom management checklist.

In her book, *Dare to Lead*, Brené Brown (2018) notes that vulnerability is not the sign of weakness that we often perceive it to be. It's quite the opposite. Brown mentions that today's researchers often seek to examine one's willingness to be vulnerable as a means of measuring one's courage. So let your guard down, embrace the idea of being vulnerable in front of your students, and discover a sense of courage that you never knew was sitting dormant inside of you!

FAMILY ENGAGEMENT

Another critical part of becoming a teacher leader is displaying the willingness to go above and beyond as it relates to engaging students' families as well as the community as a whole. Building a successfully strong relationship with students requires more work than just a fist bump on the way into the classroom each morning. While a classroom greeting is excellent and a practice I highly recommend, that action alone will not be enough to ensure a strong bond between you and the child. In order to gain the trust necessary to formulate a relationship, the student wants to know that you're invested in their world. Kids are incredibly smart and can sense when a teacher is laying it on thick to appear interested in their life. Do you care about their home life? Their parents, guardians, siblings? Do you care about where they're hanging out after school and with whom? You can do this, but it requires work. By regularly engaging in conversations with families as well as community leaders, you will demonstrate your innate desire to best meet the needs of each child in front of you.

FAMILY ENGAGEMENT

As teachers, we have a lot on our plate. We rightly have to prioritize our to-do lists daily. As such, there may be items at the bottom of our list that continually get pushed aside to another. I can't blame you. I've been guilty of doing just that myself. Unfortunately, I have seen teachers putting parent/guardian toward the bottom of their daily to-do lists. I encourage you to avoid putting off such a vital component of engagement. Engagement with families goes a long way in ensuring a collaborative effort to meet the needs of the student. Luckily, there are many ways to communicate effectively with parents and guardians.

Newsletter

One of my favorite ways of communicating with family throughout the school year is through a bi-weekly newsletter disseminated by way of email. Every other Friday, I send out "Mr. McHale's ELA Update" to my students and their families. Within the newsletter will be an overall welcome message, links to instructional materials, study guides, as well as pertinent information for the next two weeks of class.

It seems like an overwhelming project to undertake, but I assure you it's simple and acts as a highly effective means of communication. Most of my parent-initiated emails come by way of a reply from the newsletter. Why the uptick in parent emails (mostly positive but some undoubtedly expressing some concern regarding their child's work) from the newsletter? It's all about tone!

When I'm writing my newsletter, I'm always mindful of my tone of every sentence. I want this bi-weekly mailing to invoke a sense of excitement and camaraderie. The ultimate goal is to instill a sense of transparency. I want parents and guardians to know what's happening in their child's classroom at all times.

While sending a newsletter every other week can seem like a daunting task, it doesn't have to be. Utilize the template gallery of Google Docs (there are quite a few options for newsletters) to create a personalized template. Once you've spent time getting the look, feel, and organization of your newsletter down, you'll only have to update each section when it's time to release a new edition.

Here's one of my first newsletters from my first year as an eighth grade English language arts teacher:

Mr. McHale - 8th Grade Language Arts
ELA Newsletter

A Successful Term 1!
Hello again, everyone! I hope this edition of the ELA newsletter finds you and your family doing well. I can't believe that we are already a third of the way through the school year.

Overall, Term 1 was quite successful. While the transition to 8th grade may have been smoother for some than others, all students managed to show growth in at least one major area of emphasis.

As we move into Term 2, it's important for students to remember that they'll be held to higher standards as it relates to academic and behavioral expectations in my classroom. There's a lot of work to be done if students are to be adequately prepared for the challenges that await them in high school. Everyone, myself included, needs to be on the top of their game each and every day.

Parent/Teacher Conferences
I'm looking forward to meeting all of you during Parent/Teacher Conferences this week! As a reminder, all appointments are now made online. The links to sign up for a specific time slot can be found below:

Thursday/Friday Conferences: www.websitenolongeravailable.com

Monday (12/11) Conferences: www.websitenolongeravailable.com

If you are unable to attend a conference and would like an update on your child's progress, please email me at pondereducation@gmail.com. I'd be more than happy to send you an update via email or phone.

Contact Information
Email: pondereducation@gmail.com
Twitter: @pondereducation
Subscribe to my YouTube channel![1]
Phone: 867-5309

WHERE WE'VE BEEN...
As we continue working our way through Unit 2 (Drama), we have already tackled the following topics:

1. Drama
   A. Overview and Vocabulary Terms
      1. "12 Angry Men"
II. Discussed the rights of all American citizens (Bill of Rights, Rights of the Accused).
III. Discussed mass incarceration, institutionalized racism, and the problematic nature of jury trials.
IV. Assigned parts and "performed" play in class.
V. Discussed the major themes present in the play.
VI. Compared and contrasted the play's script with the Hollywood movie adaptation.
   A. Started reading Thornton Wilder's epic three-act play, *Our Town*.

WHERE WE'RE GOING…
My goal is to wrap up our 2nd unit prior to the upcoming holiday break. Students will be tasked with successfully completing two significant assessments:

I. Unit Exam
   A. A combination of multiple choice, short answer, and essay questions designed to ensure that students mastered all the objectives outlined in the unit.
II. Project-Based Assessment
   A. Students will be tasked with working collaboratively in a group setting to write a one-act play. The kids will have to write a properly formatted script that includes dialogue and stage directions.

Following the conclusion of the drama unit, we will read our first novel of the year. More information regarding our novel will be sent home in the coming weeks.

Upcoming Events

Date	Event
December 7	Mr. McHale out for the day (Curriculum Team Leader meetings)
December 8	Book Fair
December 11	1st Independent Reading Book for students in Tie-Dye and Gold classes due
December 22	Vacation begins at the conclusion of school.
January 2	School resumes

PARENT AND GUARDIAN PHONE CALLS

Aside from the distribution of a classroom newsletter, engaging directly with parents and guardians goes a long way in strengthening the bond among ourselves, a student, and their family. Effective teaching, in my opinion, requires an exemplary ability to engage with families. In doing so, you're communicating to both the student and their parents/guardians that you are fully invested in ensuring the academic and social success of the child. As a parent of two kids in public schools myself, I can tell you that it means a lot to have a teacher initiating contact regarding the performance of my little ones.

Unfortunately, some teachers may have a negative connotation associated with parent phone calls. That's because we too often focus on calling home when there is something wrong. We are calling because a child refused to behave or work well in the classroom. It's never fun to make those types of phone calls. No one wants to tell a parent that their kid is struggling in some fashion. Likewise, no parent looks forward to constant negative feedback. I'd go so far as to say that the frequent negative feedback only increases the divide that typically may exist between teachers and parents/guardians.

How can we change the mindset of the parent phone call?

Honestly, we will always have to make those calls that we wished we didn't have to make. We are, after all, working with young children who are still unable to fully process their complex emotions. However, there are two things that I'd ask we consider when discussing the future of parent phone calls:

1. *Balance the Bad with some Good*

Of course, there will be times that we will have to call the parents/guardians of a student when we wish we didn't have to. But that doesn't mean it has to be a call hyper-focused on the negative actions of their child. Regardless of how they may perform or act in your classroom setting, there is inherent good within each student. So while you may be calling in response to a particular incident, use the established line of communication to convey one of the many positives you're still noticing. It'll go far in showing parents/guardians that you will never define a child by one bad decision or class.

In my calls with parents, I enjoy starting the conversation off with something positive. It will help, should parents and guardians begin the call on the defensive. Some parents and guardians may have had negative experiences with teachers in the past, either themselves directly or with their other children. As a result, they may begin the call ready and willing to defend their child (and rightfully so) and push back against your perception of the incident in question. To negate the chances of having a conversation go off the deep end right off the bat, I love to use the start of the phone call to express my appreciation for their child as well as their willingness to spend time out of their busy day to talk.

Sample Phone Call Script
Teacher: Good morning, Mr./Mrs. LastName. My name is Ryan McHale, and I am <Insert Child's Name> English language arts teacher.
Parent: Oh, no.
Teacher: Thank you for taking time out of your day to chat with me for a few moments. I want to say that I'm truly enjoying working with <Insert Child's Name>. <Insert appropriate pronoun> is <Insert positive feedback here>.
Parent: Oh, thank you! That's great to hear.
Teacher: My pleasure! That said, I did want to inform you of something that happened at school today...
After you've communicated your concerns, be mindful of the parent/guardian response. Truly listen to their reaction and concerns. Be sure to acknowledge their feedback as well. Again, it takes a willingness of all parties involved to work collaboratively and transparently to help our students be successful.
Teacher: I thank you for your time and your feedback regarding this issue. We both know that <Insert Child's Name> has the ability to do great things, both inside and outside the classroom. I'm looking forward to our continued partnership this year as we help <Insert Child's Name> demonstrate academic and social growth. Please never hesitate to reach out if you have any questions, comments, or concerns. End Call.

MAKING THE MOST OF PARENT-TEACHER CONFERENCES

I'm just going to put this right out here for all to see. I absolutely love parent-teacher conferences. I know those days can be incredibly long, especially if they occur at night after a long day of school. And yes, they can certainly produce feelings of anxiety as we wonder what parents and/or guardians have to say about our class. Yet, there is something fantastic about these meetings.

These conferences allow us to speak candidly about a student with the people who love them the most. We are all there for the same reason. We're gathered around a table (or a cluster of epically small student desks) to speak about how to best meet the academic and social needs of a young person with endless potential. For those few minutes, we are all on the same page and outlining future goals for the student in question. It's a wonderful thing.

Of course, the quality of each parent or guardian interaction depends on several variables, some of which are outside our control. However, there are certainly steps that we can take on our end to give us the best chance for a highly productive parent-teacher conference.

Identify Parents/Guardians Most Likely to Attend and Reach Out to Those Who May Be Unable to Visit

Thanks to the wonderful world of technology, it has become increasingly easy to have a firm grasp on which parents and/or guardians are most likely to plan a visit on conference night. Gone are the days of the true "open house." In the past, many schools would literally open their doors as parents would file in and head toward the classroom of a particular teacher. Educators would peek outside their door to see a swarm of parents outside waiting to catch your ear as to the performance of their child. It could undoubtedly be anxiety-inducing simply because you had to mentally prepare for the possibility of any student's parents to arrive. With a shift toward the use of digital technology, however, such uncertainty is unlikely to rear its head.

Today, most schools are affording parents and guardians with the opportunity to sign up for set times to meet with individual teachers. In doing so, schools are giving teachers time to review the list of scheduled attendees and plan accordingly. I cannot tell you enough that knowing who will be stopping by your classroom significantly reduces nerves and helps in the planning of each meeting. As soon as the sign-up website goes live, I am checking the site at the end of every school day leading up to the event.

As great as it may be to have an online platform to help schedule parent-teacher conferences, it's important to remember that it still won't be enough to ensure that every parent and/or guardian is 1) made aware of conference dates and 2) given an equitable opportunity to respond. I have noticed that many parents today are forced to either take on odd-hour jobs or work multiple jobs that makes scheduling conferences incredibly challenging. Many parents and guardians cannot afford to take time off from work to attend these meetings.

And what about single parents? Or single parents with multiple children? While I may never know the day-to-day struggles of a single parent, I can surely empathize. I think of all the times that I was lucky enough to have my wife by my side to help take on parental responsibility. We must understand that parents who do not respond to (or, in some cases, decline) an invitation do not love their children any less than the parents who respond to conference sign-up emails within a minute of receiving the 'DING' notification on their electronic device.

If you are struggling with getting parents into the building for conferences, consider doing what it is we do for every child in our classroom: meet them where they are! You can always offer to talk over the phone after school hours or engage in professional dialogue through email. Perhaps you can schedule a time to meet during your prep period one day if it's the only opportunity for a parent or guardian to visit. Don't be afraid to think outside the box. Offer alternatives to the structured parent-teacher conference schedule! After all, two-way communication with parents and guardians has, and in my humble opinion, will always be a crucial part in ensuring student success. As parent-teacher night approaches, you may wish to consider the following tips to make the night go as smoothly as possible:

Have Student Work and Data Easily Accessible

With the majority of pertinent information regarding student performance being widely accessible via the internet, this portion of conference prep has become exponentially easier. In previous years, I'd accumulate data and place everything into a binder. Information was separated by class with each roster organized in alphabetical order. It was a monotonous task but one that proved helpful during any conference or team meeting dealing with student academic and social performance.

Today, however, everything that you needed any of the aforementioned meetings is right at your fingertips thanks to the ever-changing world of education technology. If you have an online grade book, you can pull up all data related to a child almost instantaneously. But that doesn't mean you no longer have to consider the pitfalls of such technology. As we all know from our time in the classroom, technology has a funny way of failing you at the very moment you need it most. I can't tell you how nervous I tend to get prior to a lesson, presentation, etc. that relies heavily on technology. I've come to make sure I'm not dependent on working tech in order to complete the mission at hand.

When I'm planning for a student's conference, I am typically going to ensure that I have previous state standardized test scores (MCAS - the Massachusetts Comprehensive Assessment System), the most up-to-date class average, any behavioral incidents, and at least one writing sample. Since time is of the essence during these in-and-out meetings, I want to have everything I need to have a productive conversation with each parent/guardian. Therefore, I will print the items I need and place them in an organized binder with a designated section per each of my five classes. At times, there may be a parent/guardian who arrives unscheduled, and, in those few cases, I'll rely on technology to pull up any necessary supplemental information.

Ultimately, the more you're able to prepare for parent-teacher conferences, the better. You'll be able to adequately prepare for the night's event, which will, in turn, increase your confidence level heading into the meetings.

. . .

Avoid Focusing Simply on the Negative

When the time comes to begin preparing for parent-teacher conferences, it can be tempting to go all-in on the parents/guardians of a student who you have perceived to be underperforming or misbehaving. Please resist this urge. While it certainly is the appropriate time to express concerns, I'd ask you to consider refraining from centering the conversation on negativity. Despite the performance of the child to that point, you cannot honestly tell me that it's impossible for you to communicate the good of the student to their parent(s)/guardians(s). If that's the case, you're simply not looking hard enough.

If you find yourself looking forward to a conference simply because you're thrilled at the thought of dishing out a plate full of negativity, I'd ask you to take a moment to reflect and consider the following:

- *Will this conference be the first time the parent(s) and/or guardian(s) will be hearing from you and your barrel of bad news? If so, why?*
- *Who will genuinely be centered in this discussion? You and your unhappiness, or the student in need of additional support?*
- *What do you believe will ultimately come of the conversation if all you did was focus on what the child may be doing wrong?*
- *How will the conversation affect your relationship with the student and your ability to work collaborative with the student and family to make necessary changes?*
- *Do I have any examples of positive academic and/or social performance? If not, why? What can I discuss that'll show the positive side of the child that everyone at the table knows exists?*

ONE ALTERNATIVE TO PARENT/TEACHER CONFERENCES

Consider having students create portfolios of their work leading up to parent-teacher conferences. Within each portfolio will be a collection of graded work along with teacher-provided feedback. Also, the portfolios will contain student answers to questions such as:

- *What have I learned thus far in class?*
- *In what areas of class have I found the most significant success?*
- *In what areas of class am I displaying consistent growth?*
- *In what areas of class am I still working toward achieving mastery?*
- *What is my current plan of action for the rest of the school year as it relates to this class?*

The creation of student portfolios now gives you some options heading into parent-teacher conferences. You can offer to allow the student to sit in on the meeting and present their portfolio to their family. Alternately, you can show the portfolio to parents/guardians if the student is not permitted to attend per (outdated and archaic) school policy. Finally, you can connect with any parents and guardians who are unable to attend in-person conferences to ensure they see their child's portfolio and offer to answer any questions they may have. It's certainly an alternative worth exploring!

LET YOUR VOICE BE HEARD

Starting your teaching career is scary, no doubt about it. It can be intimidating to speak openly on behalf of yourself and your students. As a new educator, imposter syndrome is real. You'll look around at all the teachers in your building who have been there and done that. You'll question your teaching abilities. You'll probably think you have nothing new to bring to the table. Resist the temptation to remain silent.

When you are feeling less than confident in your skills as a new educator, remember one thing: you were hired for a reason. The administrative team in your building brought you on board because they saw something in you. They saw passion. They saw a willingness to go to great lengths to help your students find success inside and outside the classroom. Your administrators hired you with confidence because they knew that you were going to be an agent of change. As Angie Thomas wrote in the best-selling Young Adult novel, *The Hate U Give* (2017), "What's the point in having a voice if you're gonna be silent in those moments you shouldn't be?"

We're at a crossroads in education. We're so heavily focused on data, technology integration, grit, growth mindset, and *<insert other education buzzwords here>*. All of these aspects of teacher certainly have their place. I'm never going to debate that fact. However, those issues are only parts of a much larger puzzle. Step back and take a second to look at the big picture. What's missing? What's missing from the educational experience we are providing today's youth? It's equity. Racial equity. Gender equity. Equity for students receiving special education support. Socioeconomic equity. The inequities that have existed in education from day one continue to plague our system today. No data team, new laptop, or anti-bullying program will be successful until we address inequity. You were meant to be an educator because you have the desire to help bring about change. Don't wait. Remember, students don't have that luxury.

MAKE SOME NOISE RIGHT OFF THE BAT

Over the years, as I've continued working toward earning a license in school administration, I have emphasized learning the ins and outs of the hiring process. Of course, many folks will have different needs based on building openings as well as a school's climate and culture, but there was one thing that appears to be a must for all hiring administrators. Principals are on the lookout for agents of change! They want a difference-maker. There's no time for tentativeness. Schools are looking for new staff members to come in and create waves of positivity.

When I was first hired as a classroom teacher, my new principal noticed my background in political science, thanks to my time at Suffolk University in Boston. It just so happened that the school needed another advisor to the building's Student Council. I accepted the invitation to help lead to the student-run organization right away. It was certainly right up my alley. I used the opportunity to highlight what I can bring to the table as it relates to helping build a positive school climate and strengthening student-teacher relationships.

At the time of my hiring, the school in which I was employed was looking for ways to increase our MCAS standardized test scores. While I am, by no means, a supporter of high stakes testing, I believe that if we have to take this test then let's help students build their intrinsic motivation to crush the damn thing. So, in my very first year as a classroom teacher, my Student Council co-advisor and I decided to shake things up. We decided to film a video that would serve as a 25-30 minute PSA on how to succeed at taking this test and how it will ultimately prove beneficial to each student. We aimed to strike a mix of seriousness with the absurd. To get kids thinking while also sharing a few good laughs. Our goal? To have kids leaving the auditorium, knowing that they are more than capable of dominating the MCAS!

Our finished product was an interesting blend of NBC "The More You Know"-esque ads and Saturday Night Live sketches. I allowed myself to become completely vulnerable throughout the shooting of the film. I danced. I sang (horribly out of tune). I cracked jokes that were wholly hit or miss. But I think we managed to deliver on our goal of inspiring all of our students. That's all that matters.

During the film, I made it known to all the kids watching that they could demonstrate their mastery of the grade-level curricula in front of them. I did it with my voice and a smile. I was the new guy, and here I was spreading positive energy and excitement throughout the building. I had students from other clusters swinging by my room to say hello. I had parents emailing me about the video. I had peers giving thanks and congratulations for a job well done.

I'll be the first to admit…it wasn't easy. As an introvert, the idea of putting myself out there (especially so early in my career) caused much anxiety. However, I knew that my principal took a chance on me because of my potential to bring about a positive change within the building. While others doubted my readiness to jump into the classroom, she never wavered. She saw something in me and knew that I could positively influence the lives of countless students should I be hired. So, I took a deep breath and jumped right in. I encourage you to do the same!

FILL A VOID…START A CLUB!

As you become more acclimated to your building and the needs of your students and community, you will certainly notice deficit areas as it relates to special interest clubs. When I first started teaching, my school was a Grade 5-7 building with our eighth graders moving into a separate building to prepare for the challenges of high school that soon awaited them. Years later, it was announced that, due to the construction of a new elementary school within the district, the fifth grade would move to the new building and the eighth graders would come back to the middle school building, making it your typical Grade 6-8 middle school model. As soon as the move happened, it became abundantly clear that we, as a school community, were not completely prepared to assist our eighth-grade students in many social aspects.

Months before the move happened, an 8th grade ELA position opened, and I was able to make the move from sixth grade to eighth. I was ecstatic to work with our oldest students and help prepare them for success at the high school level. It didn't take long to fully grasp the fact that these children were experiencing far more personal challenges than my sixth graders had in the past. During my unit on spoken word poetry, students, through brilliant, personal verse, brought me inside the mind of the eighth-grade student. It was eye-opening.

As I perused their work, one common theme was repeatedly jumping out at me. Over a dozen students had written about sexual orientation. Many mentioned having to bottle up their truths. Many were openly stating they identified as an LGBTQIA student. They mentioned feeling alone as they were unable to speak with a family member, nor did they feel entirely welcomed and safe within the confines of school. As someone striving to be a change agent, I knew something had to be done to provide support and assistance to these wonderful, young kids.

I spoke at length with a dear friend who was also one of the building's guidance counselors. We devised a plan to pitch the creation of our school's first-ever Gay-Straight Alliance (GSA) organization. At this time, GSAs were rapidly growing at the middle school level due to the increase in harmful incidents against the LGBTQIA community. We gathered applicable data to strengthen our case and met with our administrative team. We were taken aback (in the best possible way) at the support we received regarding our proposal to head up a GSA.

Within a day, we were given the green light to launch the group officially.

There are simply no words to describe the looks that came across the faces of many of our students who were feeling vulnerable and marginalized -- not just in school, but in society as a whole. There was a sense of immediate relief, knowing that there would be a safe place to meet with like-minded individuals. Whether those other students were a part of the LGBTQIA community themselves or simply a willing accomplice in the mission to increase equity, it served as a reminder to all the kids that they were not alone. It was a breathtaking moment and one that I'll never forget when I one day reflect on my time as an educator.

To this day, helping to launch a school-wide GSA has been one of my proudest accomplishments. It was a defining moment for me as an educator looking to disrupt the status quo and demonstrate to the kids of the school that the adults in the building truly cared about their social-emotional well-being. While our GSA was not an activist organization per se, we were a group that helped move the needle as it relates to understanding the plight of LGBTQIA students at the middle school level. We also provided dozens of kids with an organized space to convene, talk, laugh, cry, and find strength through shared life experiences.

It doesn't matter what kind of club you may one day decide to form. Just know that if and when you do go that route, you'll be positively impacting the lives of the students who join in ways you'll never forget. If you come to notice the need for a particular student organization, you can be assured that many students will be entirely grateful for the safe space you've created.

SECTION THREE
Avoid

One of the most disconcerting notions that surround education these days, particularly on social media sites such as Instagram, Pinterest, and Twitter is the idea that our job is filled with rainbows and sunshine daily. In my opinion, this take is highly disingenuous. In fact, it's downright dangerous for the psyche of teachers. Belief in such a fallacy will inevitably lead to disappointment. Why? Because our job (teacher, administrator, guidance counselor) is a roller-coaster of emotions. Make no mistake about it. You will experience the highest of highs and the lowest of lows in ten months. It's reality, and you need to know it.

Toxic positivity, "the belief that if you just stay positive it will allow you to power through whatever obstacles you encounter" (Ellwood, 2018), is a real concern for new teachers and career changers. The pictures posted by teachers online tell one story. The reality often tells another. I can't help but think back to my own Facebook page. It's my personal photo album, and I'm always sharing photos of my family. The majority of the pictures uploaded tell the story of the happiest of families. Two kids full of joy, smiling widely during the latest family outing. If you didn't know any better, you'd think I had a pair of angels.

What didn't I show?

I didn't show the temper tantrums. I neglected to discuss the meltdown in the car that required me to pull over on the highway. The picture of my wife and me shedding tears after a stressful day? It doesn't exist. I cherry-pick what I share. We all do. Teachers included.

So be careful of the overly positive and understand that what's being shown is intentional. If you get it in your mind that what you see is what you'll get when jumping into the classroom, you'll inevitably be filled with frustration, sadness, and even anger. Eventually, you'll find yourself questioning your work, and you'll be one of the teachers who leaves the profession within their first five years.

It doesn't have to be this way.

The key is to be able to identify, understand, and carefully negotiate through the turmoil that'll rise during your first few years on the job. And so, Section 3 will discuss those negative parts of the job and what can be done to improve those issues and continue onward in your journey to positively impact the lives of your students and community. It may not be pretty, but that's life. And it's education.

AVOID THE PERPETUATION OF RACIAL INEQUITIES

Throughout your teacher preparation program, you have probably come to notice that there's much of the same discussion over and over again. You've probably thought that your prep program could have been cut in half due to the repetitive nature of the content. You're not alone. The fact is that many aspects of education have remained the same for quite some time. And that's a problem.

The solution? Well, it all depends on what you feel to be the most pressing issue facing education today. As I've continued to learn and grow as an educator, there has been one constant epidemic that has, without fail, caused undue harm to far too many children. And while many will agree that it's a pressing issue in need of addressing, few will take actionable steps to improve the system.

So what exactly is the problem bogging down our schools? Inequity.

I see the stagnation of education being about affording the best educational opportunities to certain populations -- white, male, and economically advantaged. It is here where the status quo must be dismantled.

As a new teacher, it may sound as though this is a task far too large to tackle. And, without a doubt, it certainly isn't an easy one. However, if you can become aware of the systemic inequities plaguing our system now, you'll be better equipped to provide students in your classroom (and in your school) with an equitable education.

With your desire to join us in the field of education, it's clear you've done so knowing that challenges that lay ahead and wanting, more than anything, to push past those potential stumbling blocks to help students learn and grow. So let's talk about how racial inequities are perpetuating the achievement gap and how, through your willingness to engage in difficult conversations and work, you can step right into the classroom and make a difference.

WHITE PRIVILEGE

Today, white students (especially able-bodied, heterosexual white males) are continuing to reap the benefits of a system that was designed with their future success in mind. Students of color, on the other hand, are fighting tooth and nail for opportunities. Yes, it's a privilege. It's a White Privilege. And it's all around us. And it must be stopped.

An exact definition of white privilege has been notoriously challenging to pin down. However, a seminal piece from Peggy McIntosh (1988) titled, "Unpacking the Invisible Knapsack," issued the most widely-accepted definition by referencing the concept as

An invisible package of unearned assets that I can count on cashing in each day, but about which I was "meant" to remain oblivious. White privilege is like an invisible weightless knapsack of special provisions, maps, passports, codebooks, visas, clothes, tools, and blank checks.

The idea of white privilege, regardless of whether or not there existed an explicit definition, has always been continually permeating throughout American society.

In 1896, the United States Supreme Court ruled in the landmark case, *Plessy v. Ferguson* (163 U.S. 537), that racial segregation, "the practice of restricting people to certain circumscribed areas of residence or to separate institutions (e.g., schools, churches) and facilities (parks, playgrounds, restaurants, restrooms) on the basis of race or alleged race" (Encyclopedia Britannica, 2019) was legal. The country, by way of the court's decision, signified its acceptance of white privilege. While perhaps insisting on a society that was "separate, but equal," the United States, just thirty-one years removed from the abolition of slavery, was still maintaining that one race was superior over all others.

However, the decision issued by the country's highest court in 1954's *Brown v. Board of Education* (347 U.S. 483) virtually eliminated *Plessy's* allowance of legal segregation. The case brought the issue of racism in America to the forefront of the nation's conscience, particularly within the world of education. The court's decision, however, failed to eradicate racism from all societal constructs. Instead, white privilege went underground. It attempted to morph into an unseen form of racial discrimination. However, research such as the work of Francis E. Kendell (2002) shows that white citizens of the United States are (and have always been) afforded considerable advantages in all aspects of life, particularly when it comes to receiving an equitable education.

Much of the research surrounding the idea of white privilege in education has put on a spotlight on eye-opening themes: white teachers' perceptions of students of color, whitewashed curricula, inequitable access to technology and supplies, and the white fragility that continues to make the eradication of white privilege difficult.

Statistically speaking, it's more probable than not that the majority of you with this book in your hand are white. It's a harsh truth. Over 80% of current educators in the United States are white (Department of Education, 2016). Being white does not mean that you cannot play a significant role in the destruction of white privilege within education, but it does mean you have work to do. All white educators do - myself included. We need to understand the history of institutionalized racism within education, notice how white privilege manifests itself within our curriculum, and take action to level the playing field for students of color.

. . .

Racial Inequity Remains

Now, if you think that racism can't possibly still exist in 2019, I'd ask you to consider current statistics as it relates to academic performance, disciplinary rates, dress code issues, and access to Honors level courses. Let's briefly delve into some of these eye-popping statistics to understand the sense of urgency.

Academic Performance

- Achievement gaps between students of color and their white peers continue to persist. Despite considerable "effort" from the U.S. government to work to close these gaps, the rate of improvement over time is simply embarrassing. Why do we continue to allow 40% of classrooms with students of color as the majority to receive below-grade level work whereas only 12% of classrooms with white students as the majority are faced with the same reprehensible education (Cantor, 2018)?

Disciplinary Rates

- Researchers at Princeton University recently released a study that showed Black students were far more likely to be disciplined compared to their white peers (Riddle & Sinclair, 2019). According to their research, students of color were nearly four times more likely to receive an out-of-school suspension than white students. Black students were also far more likely to be arrested in-school, referred to law enforcement, or even expelled from school altogether.

Access to Honors and AP Level Courses

- The Department of Education Office of Civil Rights released a report (2014) that detailed the racial disparities related to High School Honors and AP opportunities for students of color:
- Only 27% of Black and Latino students were enrolled in at least one AP course.
- Black, Latino, and Indigenous students continue to have less access to higher-level math and science courses compared to their white peers.
- Indigenous students have less access to English language instruction programs (only 81% of Indigenous students English language learners receiving adequate instruction).
- Students of color are far more likely to be retained.

As I reflect on these statistics, I wonder how big a role teacher perception has to the academic and social expectations of students of color. Wright (2015) found that Black teachers have much less negative views of Black student behavior than do white teachers. Interestingly enough, Wright's research also showed that Black teachers' expectations of white students were roughly the same as the expectations they held for Black students. The bottom line is simple: Being matched with a teacher of a similar race means much more to students of color than it does for white students. Quite the privilege to have, no?

Two ways in which our system can become much more equitable, it seems, would be to place a considerable amount of effort into hiring more educators of color while simultaneously working with white educators to overcome what DiAngelo (2018) calls **white fragility** — the defensiveness that white people feel when challenged racially. White fragility, as DiAngelo notes, will often manifest itself through anger, confrontation, and eventual silence, making productive conversation and necessary action almost impossible to obtain.

So, how can you, as a new educator, help bring racial equity to the education of the students in front of you? First, diversify your literature and content to highlight the work of people of color. In Math and Science courses, discuss the contributions to those fields from people of color. In Social Studies, expand your lessons beyond the basics of slavery, Civil Rights, and Martin Luther King, Jr. In English, select literature that is written by people of color and prominently features main characters of color.

Helping to improve racial equity is a must. Everyone in education bears the responsibility of doing so. The beautiful thing to remember is that adding works of people of color or selecting works of literature that feature a person of color as the story's protagonist only takes a conscientious effort. Start reviewing your curriculum now. How diversified is the content? What can be improved? Begin looking for new resources. You'd be pleasantly surprised by the amount of free content available online. I'd recommend taking a look through TeachingTolerance.org. If, for example, you're an ELA teacher thinking of a new class novel, ask your administrator or curriculum leader. Should the answer be no, don't give up? Continue doing whatever it takes to provide your students with the education they deserve. It can be done. Here's a look at the steps I took to bring Angie Thomas's phenomenal book, *The Hate U Give*, into my classroom.

Adding The Hate U Give to the 8th Grade Curriculum: A Case Study

After spending much of the summer of 2018 immersed in research regarding racial inequities in education, I was determined to go back into the classroom and shake things up. I knew it had to be done, and I was going to make it happen come hell or high water.

As an eighth grade English teacher, I thought that the most effective way to bring about racial equity was through the literature I chose to read and discuss with my students. Reflecting on previous school years, I realized just how whitewashed the curriculum had become. An audit of the novels, short stories, and poems I had been using I class for years revealed a truth that I should have been more aware of from day one. The vast majority of all works was either written by a white person or contained a white main character and/or hero. So, I decided it was time for a change.

As I continually racked my mind over the last few weeks of summer, I struggled to choose works of literature to add to the curriculum, not because there were no options — quite the opposite. There were so many wonderful potential additions, and I did not want to make the wrong decision.

I decided that the best course of action would be to put the decision in the hands of the one group of stakeholders whose voice frequently goes unheard: the students. I decided that I would survey all students during the first week of school to identify the books that THEY would like to read, analyze, and discuss together.

A coy smile cracks across my face as I think back to the day I gave my students the "Class Novel Survey" through a simple Google Form. They were caught by surprise. One young lady timidly raised her hand and asked, "Wait, so you're saying that we can have a say in what we read in ELA?"

"Absolutely," I responded firmly.

"What's the catch?" another student asked.

"No catch," I stated with confidence. "I have decided that I want you all to have a say in what we cover in class. What kind of books do YOU like? What kind of characters do YOU want to live vicariously through? What themes do YOU wish to dissect? We're a team here, and we all have a say."

With that, the kids got to work on the survey.

That night, I spent time going over the results. It was clear that there was one runaway winner. Over 85% of ALL surveys had listed Angie Thomas's groundbreaking novel, *The Hate U Give*, as a top choice for a classroom novel. I wasn't the least bit shocked. I had read the book twice already and fallen in love with the story of Starr Carter and her fight for justice following the murder of her dear friend at the hands of a police officer. In addition, there was considerable buzz for the film adaptation that was, at the time, only two months away from its release.

However, I also knew that the book contained foul language and brief moments of sexual innuendo. How would the administration react? Would some parents put up a fight regarding its inclusion in the eighth grade ELA curriculum? Would it be worth the hassle to bring in a book that had already been banned by many districts across the country? I only had an answer to the last question…

Would it be worth the possibility of getting in trouble?

Oh yes. It most certainly would.

I was determined to make this novel addition happen. I knew that this book would open the door to tremendous dialogue in the classroom. Conversely, I was aware that attempting to bring about change in the public school setting can take a frustratingly long time. My students didn't have time. So, I decided to take matters into my own hands.

Step 1: Research and Plan

I knew that to make this monumental change to the curriculum, that I would have to take my time and do the homework. I spent a considerable amount of time re-reading the novel, identifying desired student outcomes, and aligning everything to the Common Core Standards. While I wasn't going to seek approval from the administration or the district office, I wanted to be confident in how I would respond to higher-ups should I be questioned on the choice of book down the line.

While we as educators have an obligation from our administrators to uphold the curriculum frameworks in front of us, we are still afforded autonomy in how we go about teaching the required material. I found the literature choices that had become staples of the eighth-grade curriculum to be whitewashed in nature. Despite a rapidly evolving demographic, changes to the novels we were using in class were not. As a result, many students were unable to read stories that include characters who looked like them, acted like them, and were forced to face and overcome similar obstacles in life.

Once I had created my unit (complete with target objectives and alignment to the Massachusetts frameworks) and had a clear and compelling argument for the need to create a more culturally responsive curriculum, I tucked them away in the top drawer of my desk and set about attempting to acquire a class set of Angie Thomas's *The Hate U Give*.

Game on.

Step 2: Create a DonorsChoose Project

If you're unfamiliar with DonorsChoose, definitely take some time to view their website and understand their mission. On the site, you, as an educator, can request items for your students, classroom, and/or school. From there, individual citizens can view your proposed projects and donate to the cause. Once your project becomes fully funded, your requested items will be sent directly to your school!

Some schools are not thrilled with the idea of their teachers requesting financial support from outside donors. Honestly, it's more than likely a matter of not wanting to appear unwilling to give their faculty what they need for their students to be successful. If that's the case in your district, I'm sorry to hear that.

The truth is that there's only so much money in school budgets to go around. School districts should understand that a teacher's desire to raise funds for supplies through DonorsChoose is not a slight against the district. It's much bigger than that. It's not at attempt to circumvent the wishes of a school district. It's an understanding that the distribution of funds in education as a whole is inequitable. Therefore, creative measures have to be taken to secure the tools necessary to assist in students finding academic and social success while in your class.

So if you're a building administrator or a part of the Central Office staff, please allow your teachers to utilize a site such as DonorsChoose to help meet the diverse needs of the students in front of them. It's not about you. It's about the kids.

Step 3: Reach Out to Parents

One of the things that I learned early on in education was that the students and their families were, for lack of a better term, our customers. It was our job to provide them with the services they deserved. If we're going to go down that road, then I'd be remiss if I didn't say that "the customer is always right." As a result, I felt as though I would be less likely to get pushback from the district if I had the backing of the students and families.

I got to work by writing a letter to parents and guardians. The correspondence contained my reasoning for adding *The Hate U Give* to the curriculum as well as all the intended learning outcomes for students. As there was considerable noise throughout social media related to the banning of T.H.U.G. from school districts across the country, I aimed to address the concerns of those misinformed districts. My goal was ultimately to gain the trust of parents and guardians. I wanted them to trust me to take their children on this exploration of systemic racism, white privilege, and social justice. Below is a brief snippet of the letter sent to parents and guardians:

While I believe the book to be one of the best Young Adult novels released in the last decade, it is not without controversy. There have been a number of school districts around the country that attempted to ban the book due to language, innuendo, and the highlighting of youth activism. However, this book, in my humble opinion, is exactly what our 8th grade students need to be reading, analyzing, and openly discussing.

Due to the content of the book, as well as the discussions that'll undoubtedly occur in class, I am requesting that all parents and guardians sign and return this form that'll give your child permission to participate in this upcoming book study.[1]

To end the letter, I decided to attach a copy of a blog post I had previously written for the website dedicated to my podcast, Pondering Education. The posting contained my reasoning for wanting eighth-grade students to read *The Hate U Give* as well as highlight the common core and social-emotional learning standards covered by the reading of this phenomenal text. Here's a look at the original post I wrote:

With all the controversy surrounding *The Hate U Give*'s inclusion in public school classrooms, it's not surprising that administrators may initially flinch at the prospect of teachers tackling this memorable novel with eighth grade students. However, I firmly believe that the book is exactly what needs to be read, meticulously analyzed, and thoughtfully discussed with kids on the cusp of high school.

Why?

Eighth grade is a pivotal year for students as they are academically and socially preparing for the challenges that await them in high school. This is the academic year in which students should be thoughtfully pushed out of their bubble in an effort to expand their level of empathy prior to departing middle school.

COMMON CORE STANDARDS

If you're an educator looking to bring a book, or any academic resource, into your classroom, you'll want to be sure to have a list of standards that will be covered because of the addition of the resource into your curriculum. For example, here is a list of just a few of the Common Core Standards (National Governors Association Center for Best Practices and Council of Chief State School Officers, 2010) that you'll meet if reading *The Hate U Give* with your eighth-grade students:

- **CCSS.ELA-LITERACY.RL.8.2**
- Determine a theme or central idea of a text and analyze its development over the course of the text, including its relationship to the characters, setting, and plot; provide an objective summary of the text.
- **CCSS.ELA-LITERACY.RL.8.3**
- Analyze how particular lines of dialogue or incidents in a story or drama propel the action, reveal aspects of a character, or provoke a decision.

- CCSS.ELA-LITERACY.RL.8.6
- Analyze how differences in the points of view of the characters and the audience or reader (e.g., created through the use of dramatic irony) create such effects as suspense or humor.
- CCSS.ELA-LITERACY.RL.8.7
- Analyze the extent to which a filmed or live production of a story or drama stays faithful to or departs from the text or script, evaluating the choices made by the director or actors.
- CCSS.ELA-LITERACY.SL.8.1
- Engage effectively in a range of collaborative discussions (one-on-one, in groups, and teacher-led) with diverse partners on grade 8 topics, texts, and issues, building on others' ideas and expressing their own clearly.

SOCIAL-EMOTIONAL LEARNING

Although many districts across the country are still developing standards to align with Social-Emotional Learning domains, the state of Illinois has recently released a comprehensive set of Social/Emotional Learning Standards (Illinois State Board of Education, 2018). I'd highly recommend referring to these standards by discussing your wish to add a new resource to your class. Here are a few of the aforementioned standards that I believed were worth mentioning to administrators when proposing adding *The Hate U Give* to my curriculum:

GOAL 1: DEVELOP SELF-AWARENESS AND SELF-MANAGEMENT SKILLS TO ACHIEVE SCHOOL AND LIFE SUCCESS.
1A — Identify and manage one's emotions and behavior.
Explain the consequences of different forms of communicating one's emotions.
GOAL 2: USE SOCIAL-AWARENESS AND INTERPERSONAL SKILLS TO ESTABLISH AND MAINTAIN POSITIVE RELATIONSHIPS.
2B — Recognize individual and group similarities and differences.

Discuss stereotyping and its negative effects for both the victim and perpetrator.

Analyze how various social and cultural groups are portrayed in the media.

Analyze how exposure to cultural diversity might either enhance or challenge your health behaviors (e.g., differing driving or eating habits, more or less psychological pressure based on differing cultural norms).

Evaluate efforts to promote increased understanding among groups.

Evaluate efforts to provide members of various groups with opportunities to work together to achieve common goals.

Evaluate how protecting the rights and responsibilities of minority student groups contributes to protecting the rights of all students.

Develop and maintain positive relationships with peers of different genders, races, and ethnic groups.

2D — Demonstrate an ability to prevent, manage, and resolve interpersonal conflicts in constructive ways.

Identify how both parties to a conflict might get their needs met.

Analyze scenarios to show how power struggles contribute to conflict.

Develop strategies for resisting negative peer pressure from different sources (e.g., best friends, casual acquaintances).

Evaluate the effectiveness of enforced resolutions vs. mutually agreed upon resolutions to conflict.

Apply conflict resolution skills to de-escalate, defuse, and/or resolve differences.

Demonstrate problem-solving techniques through participation in a simulation (e.g., a diplomatic effort to resolve an international conflict, a legislative debate).

GOAL 3: DEMONSTRATE DECISION-MAKING SKILLS AND RESPONSIBLE BEHAVIORS IN PERSONAL, SCHOOL, AND COMMUNITY CONTEXTS.

3A — Consider ethical, safety, and societal factors in making decisions.

Explain how to reduce negative outcomes in risky situations.

Explain how laws reflect social norms and affect our personal decision-making.

Examine how the depiction of violent acts in the media and entertainment might impact individuals and groups.

3C — Contribute to the well-being of one's school and community.
Identify possible service projects to do within your school.
Identify possible service projects to do within your community.
Explain how one's decisions and behaviors affect the well-being of one's school and community.
Describe how various organizations contribute to the well-being of your community.
Evaluate the impact on yourself and others of your involvement in an activity to improve your school or community.
Evaluate how you might improve your participation in a service project in your school or community.

As such, I felt compelled to turn the tables on what a curriculum had provided as a means of viewing life through windows and mirrors (Style, 1988).

Up until this point, many kids had yet to be exposed to a story that acted as a mirror. The vast majority of my students of color had only read books that were written by white authors and with white protagonists. How is it that we continually force our students of color to read a book that doesn't have a character that looks like them? That have had similar experiences as them? Sure, some books may have had a handful of characters of color here and there. But did those characters have an opportunity to be a part of resolving the conflict of the story, or were they simply an act of tokenism in action? It simply wasn't good enough.

I realized it's challenging for white students to develop a true sense of empathy for their peers of color if they've never been exposed literary works that weren't written by or included a character that looked like them. It's not because they can't. The problem is so many of our white students have never been asked to read a book that acted as a window into the lives of anyone who may not look like them or experience similar events as them. At some point, we must be willing to call whiteness by its name. Our obsession with the literary canon, a set of texts written primarily by white authors and featuring mostly white characters, needs to be called into question and examined with an equity lens. We need diverse texts in our classrooms! It starts with us. And we can make it happen so long as we never waver in our pursuit toward an equitable education for all.

AVOID AN OVERRELIANCE ON PLATITUDES

> *Platitude (n.): a remark or statement, especially one with a moral content, which has been used too often to be interesting or thoughtful (Oxford dictionary, 2019).*

One of my biggest concerns regarding the explosion of education-related discussion on social media and in local and national professional development sessions continues to be the over-reliance of platitudes serving to motivate educators. Please understand that I'm not advocating for the elimination of platitudes whatsoever. They're certainly nice to read and can help teachers center themselves after a tough day. That said, apart from making us temporarily feel good regarding our decision to join the field of education, what are they accomplishing as it relates to both student and professional learning? Are they pushing education forward? Or are they distracting us from discussing and tackling the difficult challenges facing a profession that is perpetually embattled?

EYE CANDY IN WORDS

As it relates to these educational platitudes frequently emitted across social media and conference rooms across the country, I'll admit they look nice. Those who created those masterfully created Canva pictures did a great job. It's eye candy in words. We all read them and nod our heads in general agreement with the intention of the overused statement, but then what? What are we taking away from that statement other than enjoying a temporary surge in merriment? Is there anything contained within the platitude that we can apply within our classrooms and schools that'll positively impact student achievement and teacher efficacy.

TOXIC POSITIVITY AS AN UNINTENDED CONSEQUENCE

The spreading of positivity through the use of platitudes is well-intentioned. I'm confident that those in the education world are not trying to set a trap for new teachers. They are not setting out to show the job of teaching as a warm and fuzzy place filled with sunshine on even the stormiest of days. The impact of the statements, however, can play a significant role in your long-term job satisfaction. It's the potential impact of platitudes that concerns me.

The truth of the matter is teaching is a difficult job. Yes, it's rewarding. Yes, we're helping mold the minds of the future. But, wow, is it hard. There will be days you'll leave work angry… Or in tears… Or be at a loss for words. There's no way to get around it. Some days are simply going to be better than others. It's ok to have negative feelings about teaching here and there. It's ok to question the state of things within your classroom or school. Truthfully? The internal conflict will only help in engaging others in discussing the problems you're experiencing and will hopefully lead to a collaborative effort to remedy any issues.

I fear that an overreliance on platitudes will lead to burnout and the eventual decision to leave the professional altogether. Sometimes the overused clichés that are frequently bombarding our social media timelines are painting a picture of the state of education that is misleading and not grounded in the realities of the job. When we come across such platitudes, I'd argue that we appreciate them for what they are, enjoy the brief moment of brevity, and move forward.

AVOID TAKING PERSONALLY...

...THE THINGS STUDENTS SAY.

Regardless of what grade you teach, you'll undoubtedly work alongside a child who will say something so upsetting that'll make your head spin. Perhaps you will have seen it coming. Maybe it will come as a complete shock. However it comes, it'll hit you like a Muhammed Ali punch to the temple. You'll be dazed and confused. You'll also be upset. Perhaps angry. Who am I kidding? At that moment, you'll most certainly be angry. It's human nature.

Just remember to breathe.

In and out.

In and out.

As you feel your blood pressure begin to stabilize, remember not to lash out at the child in front of you. Understand that what just happened was much more than likely a call for help rather than a personal attack on you. I know it doesn't sound fair. I know it sounds like I'm asking you to be a punching bag. I'm most certainly not.

I'm merely asking you to consider why the child is acting in such a way. Is this child overcompensating for the struggle to grasp the concept you're teaching? Is the child coming into school after listening to his parents screaming at each other all morning? Is the child struggling to adjust to new medication? Was the child previously exposed to a traumatic experience?

I can list pages worth of possible reasons for the child's behavior. The unlikeliest of reasons?

You.

When you're standing in front of a child who just made an inappropriate remark in your direction, take that breath. Calmly approach the student. Rather than antagonizing the child by loudly reprimanding them in front of their peers, ask them what's troubling them. Let them know that you're aware of the brilliance inside them and are dismayed by the out-of-left-field comment that was just tossed your way. You understand that the comment does not represent who they are or who they will one day be. Something triggered the outburst. As an educator, it's our responsibility to uncover the source of frustration. Once we do? We can work collaboratively at turning the day around for the student. However, such an approach will only work if you're able to avoid taking students' actions and comments personally.

It's not about you.

...THE THINGS PARENTS SAY.

Working with parents is a bit like working with children...only worse. I know that sounds terrible, but I mean it in the sense that parents and guardians are much less likely to back down. They'll push back. They'll criticize. They'll go to your administrator. It can be incredibly difficult.

Communicating with parents can feel the same as ice skating for the first time. You'll be incredibly tentative with an innate fear of falling. When you finally do feel as though you got the hang of it, you'll lose an edge and fall flat on your face. It'll happen. It happens to all of us. Don't fret. Just as you did on the rink all those years ago, you'll get up, dust yourself off, reflect on what happened and why, and make corrections to ensure it doesn't happen in the future.

The critical thing to remember here is that parents are...well...parents. You're discussing their child. To the person on the other end of the line, it's more than just another kid in your classroom. Honestly, it's not easy receiving unfavorable feedback regarding the progress of your own kid. I know because I've been there already...and my oldest is only seven!

Last year, when my eldest son was in first grade, he was written up twice within one week. *TWICE!* Up until that point, I couldn't even imagine him doing anything remotely along the lines of requiring administrative intervention. I felt myself growing increasingly upset thinking of a member of the school's administrative team leaning forward — perhaps down on one knee to get at eye level — and reprimand my son. *How dare they!?*

Upon reflection, I realized I had let my privilege get the best of me for a moment. I calmed myself down and made contact with the school. In the end, it was an extremely productive conversation that allowed me to see where the administrative team was coming from and what I could do to help my son better adjust to that elementary school life.

As kids get older, however, it's easy to see how conversations with parents can become dicier. We are delving into tough topics every day. Differences in opinions are going to arise. Sometimes the echoes of those classroom talks will make their way back home and elicit a response from parents. It's inevitable. The key to successfully diffusing such a situation will largely depend on how you decide to respond.

Over the years, I've been able to turn a potentially potent situation into a positive interaction that appeased the parent and helped me grow as an educator. Regardless of whether all of these steps work for you or perhaps only a couple, hopefully there is something there to help ease the anxiety you may encounter the first time you get that email from a frustrated parent and/or guardian.

Responding to Emails from Frustrated Parents: A Suggested List of Rules of Engagement

1. **Do not respond immediately.** I've made this mistake

several times throughout my career, and I'm sure I'll do it again. It's human nature to be offended by an accusatory email when you know in your heart the response was the result of misinformation. You'll want to immediately respond to clear your name of any perceived wrongdoings. However, I would encourage you to wait, reflect on the comments, and carefully begin constructing a response. I typically aim to respond to parent emails within 12-24 hours of receipt, and I would encourage you to take that time to cool down before emailing your point of view.

2. **Stay focused on the explicitly-stated concern.** Emails from parents will usually revolve around a singular event or specific concern. Perhaps a child misunderstood something you said in class, or maybe a parent feels as though your assignment is too much. Whatever the reason, it's essential to stay within the parameters of the stated issue. It is not the time to deflect and speak about the student's behavior or their previous academic performance. It may be perceived as disingenuous and an attempt to avoid the issue.

3. **It's ok to stand firm in your professional judgment.** While it is not the time to go off on a tangent and refer to unrelated issues you may have with the student, you are entirely within your rights to stand firm if you believe that there's been a misunderstanding or if you know that you've conducted yourself professionally and with the students' best interests in mind. This reminder is especially true for all educators striving to be anti-racist, anti-sexist, and anti-ableist (as I hope you are!) because pushback will be coming. Stay true to yourself and where you stand on the need to bring about equity in education.

4. **Acknowledge your own growth...and mean it.** Although we may not agree with the criticism issued by a parent or guardian, it doesn't mean that we can't turn a negative situation into a positive. Perhaps the conversation ultimately led you to a new way of thinking or drove you to

attempt a new classroom management technique. In that case, go ahead and thank the parent or guardian who initiated the conversation. Wrap up the discussion by thanking them for the engaging back-and-forth for it allowed you to see something in a new light that will ultimately help you become a better educator. However, I'd suggest only adding this last caveat provided you mean what you say. Otherwise, it may come off as disingenuous and sarcastic.

Regardless of how a negative parent or guardian email may be, it is possible to carefully craft responses that are well-planned and professional. You can undoubtedly stand firm in your beliefs as the classroom teacher while also admitting to having grown in some way as a result of the situation at hand. Uncomfortable conversations with parents may start poorly, but they certainly do not have to end that way.

...THE THINGS OTHER TEACHERS SAY.

The one thing that will never change in education is the stress that the job has on those in the field. But, I'm sure you knew that before perusing this book. We're in a high-stakes profession. Forget about test scores and other data-informed accountability measures for a moment. Let's look at the big picture. We're in the job to positively impact the lives of the children in front of us daily. Our position asks us to help bridge academic and social gaps, develop human beings of the highest moral standards, and lead in the fight for social justice and equity. There's a lot at stake!

As such, we should not be surprised by those moments where stress gets the better of our colleagues or us. It's natural. The vast majority of us (I wish I could say all, but that's unfortunately not the case) want to do right by our students, their families, and the community at large. Sometimes frustrations build up over time and, despite our best attempts to suppress said feelings, we air our grievances in a most unproductive manner. Yes, sometimes teachers openly engage in verbal or electronic confrontations. Sometimes things are said that immediately elicit a feeling of anger, sadness, or even resentment. Again, it's natural.

However, when those tense moments arise (and they will), remember that in most cases, the uncomfortable words flowing freely from the mouth of a colleague is coming from a genuinely good place. It's not about you. It may seem like it at the moment, but it's not. The frustration is more than likely the result of your peer feeling at a loss for, what they perceive to be, an inexplicable reason for being unable to provide their student(s) with the academic and social enrichment the child(ren) deserve.

As I mentioned earlier, in dealing with perceived disrespect coming from a student, it's essential to take a deep breath and dissect the situation. Why is this person feeling such aggravation? What can I do to help calm this colleague down? How can I ensure my peer that I am forever on their side and will do whatever needs to be done to help them?

...THE THINGS SAID ON SOCIAL MEDIA.

Aw, yes. We've circled the wagons here a bit as we have returned to the issue of social media. As we have previously discussed, social media has so much potential for good within the education community. From free PD opportunities to the natural formation of a Professional Learning Community, an educator can leverage the best aspects of social media to learn, grow, and reflect. That's not to say all things these mediums are without criticisms. My number one issue with frequenting social media websites is the frequent encounters with folks looking to pick a battle over every word you've typed. Sure, you can block users as you run into them, but you've already seen the harsh comments. So that begs the question…How do we work to ensure our mental health and well-being when encountering these bullies from behind a computer screen in some far off land?

Don't take it personally.

I know it's easier said than done, but we have to strive to push through the negativity that seemingly festers within sites like Twitter, Instagram, and Facebook. To do so, we have to be willing to accept that there are individuals who, like Alfred told Bruce Wayne in *The Dark Knight*, "just want to watch the world burn" (Nolan & Nolan, 2008). Those who attempt to attack your opinion without cause are trolls. Simple as that. And what's the number one rule when dealing with trolls? Don't feed them!

That said, there are still a vast majority of individuals on social media who are sincere in their inquiry as it relates to your views on education. They will seek to engage in a collegial discussion that could very well assist in your growth as an educator. In such a case, it may be worthwhile to keep the line of communication open. So how exactly can we differentiate between an internet troll and a social media user looking to share, and perhaps expand upon, their views of education? There are two things to review and consider.

1. Be sure to check the basics.

Take a look at the account's profile. Is there an actual picture of a human being, or is it blank? Is it a meme? Is it a random avatar? Most trolls will never post a picture of themselves. They'll hide behind the safety of a seemingly innocuous picture.

Do they have any followers? If they are following thousands of accounts yet have zero followers? The chances are high that this account is a troll account. When was their account established? Many times troll accounts will be started to engage in the harassment of an individual who just made what they percive to be an offensive statement. If an account has just recently opened, that should be a sign that it's a troll.

2. Take a look at their previous posts.

Sometimes reviewing the basics of an account will not be enough to ascertain the validity of an account attempting to engage you in a debate. In this case, take a brief stroll through their previous posts. Do they engage in back-and-forth dialogue with other accounts or do they seemingly have the desire to have their account act as an echo chamber in which the only voice they're interested in hearing from is their own? If this account never listens and responds to others in a meaningful way that helps move the conversation forward, it's an account that needs to be ignored. Trolls are only interested in one voice and one opinion...their own.

Most of the time, internet trolls are just overcompensating for their own shortcomings. Their harsh words are typically never personal. Ignore their comments. Block them from your account. Move forward. The journey must continue!

AVOID FALLING INTO THE TRAP OF EXTREME NEGATIVITY

I wish I could delete this chapter.
    I would love to delete this chapter. I wish I could tell you that your building is filled to capacity with educators who are still exhibiting the same zealousness of teaching that they once had when they entered the classroom.

But I can't.

If I did, I'd be just another sunshine and rainbows educator painting an unrealistic picture of the profession. What good would that do? Sure, it might get you motivated for the upcoming school year. However, the good times will certainly be tested. And what then?

What happens when you inevitably run into pockets of negativity within your building? How will the negativity ultimately be manifested? Will it even be possible to avoid becoming the next Harry Potter who's pushing back against soul-sucking dementors?

Luckily, it can be done! When things do become negative, and they will from time to time, do not assume the end is near. Do not believe that it's time to give up this whirlwind of a job. How do I know? Because I can honestly admit to following into a negativity spiral in the past. It wasn't pretty. Luckily, I had trusted colleagues willing to reach into the vortex of cynicism and pull me out. If they didn't? I sure as hell wouldn't be where I am today.

A Trip Down Negativity Lane: A Case Study

Heading into my fourth year of teaching in the building, I was feeling great. I felt as though I was comfortable in my content knowledge and pedagogy preferences. I felt as though I had established myself as an educator who had earned the respect of peers, students, and families. I had no idea that within a matter of months, I'd be feeling on edge, full of anger, and ready to throw in the towel.

As the holiday season approached during that tumultuous fourth year, the climate within the walls of the school took a dramatic shift. Whispers of unhappiness among faculty began to spread like wildfire. The whispers began to act as a subtle breeze that served only to fan the flames.

The major grievances among the displeased were with the action, or rather perceived inaction, of the administrative team as it pertained to student discipline and as well as their lack of trust in faculty and staff. I wish I could say I didn't get swept away in the tidal waves of negativity. I cannot.

I soon started to see the perceptions of others as reality, regardless of evidence. I began to become less and less engaged in the school community. I became an angry educator — one who placed blame on students rather than myself. I had lost the love I had for teaching.

As I look back upon those few months, I can't help but think of how close I was to giving it all up. I was so close to throwing in the towel and leaving the profession altogether because I lost sight of my 'why.' I forgot about the needs of my students and put the needs of myself first. Luckily, I was brought back to reality by dear friends who saw my potential to be a change agent in education. So, thank you all those who helped me out of a slump that threatened to derail my career. You know who you are!

. . .

The experience I just described is not to say that teachers never have valid reasons to become upset with the climate and culture of their school. Absolutely not. My goal in sharing this story is to show how quickly our career path can shift if we allow negative energy to envelop us.

Negativity will eventually rear its ugly head during your tenure as a classroom educator. There's no doubt about it. Negativity can be found within all aspects of our lives. When it comes, be ready for it. Have a circle of trust. Lean on them when times are troubling. Work collaboratively to reach out to those educators who may be feeling upset or stressed and see what you could do to help them regain their spark that's seemingly fading fast.

And what exactly will happen when you beat back the negativity?

You will have truly started to solidify yourself as one of your school's leading agents of change. You're saying no to negativity and displaying your willingness to create a climate and culture that's conducive to ensuring that the building is working as one to meet the academic and social needs of the students.

AVOID NEGLECTING YOUR SELF-CARE

As teachers, we work tirelessly to ensure the academic and mental well-being of our students. Frankly, it's exhausting. I mean that in the best sense of the word. Yes, it's exhausting, but it's also exhilarating. However, if we fail to engage in moments of self-care to recharge our batteries, so to speak, we will ultimately struggle to provide our students with all they need to thrive. Self-care is simply crucial in becoming a teacher leader. Burn-out is real in education, and an inability to make time for self-care opportunities only increases stress. Find what brings you peace and relaxation and make sure to set aside time for yourself. You are not selfish; you're ensuring you'll be able to meet the needs of your students the next time you step inside the classroom.

There are undoubtedly many ways to go about engaging in self-care. What do you enjoy doing in your spare time? What's a hobby that you've always wanted to take up but never had the chance? Now is the time! Make yourself available to be with the ones you love, to do the things you've wanted to do, and to free yourself from the stresses of the job momentarily.

I tend to think of two distinct categories within the realm of self-care. Both needed to be frequently tended to if we're to be the most effective teacher possible. First, there's physical self-care which refers to the proactive steps taken to ensure we're taking care of our bodies throughout the school year. Then there's emotional self-care which helps ensure we're mentally ready to tackle the day-to-day challenges of the job. Let's take a closer look at some actions we can take to ensure we are meeting our physical and emotional needs.

PHYSICAL SELF-CARE

Put an Emphasis on Sleep

- One of the most challenging aspects of teaching is the desire to do as much as possible within the confines of a given day. Whether it's staying up late grading papers or fine-tuning lesson plans, teachers are often sacrificing valuable sleep time. While our intentions are in the right place, the hard truth is that the lack of sleep is doing ourselves and our students a disservice. We can't be the best version of ourselves if we're tired. Be sure you're taking proactive steps to get enough sleep each night.
- In years past, I neglected sleep. As such, I neglected my health and my ability to function at an optimal level. I would go right from school and pick up my kids. My wife and I would be in full-on parenting mode until my son and daughter would go to bed. It was then that I decided to bust out the laptop and get to work...again. Before I knew it, it would be past midnight, and my alarm was less than six hours away from jerking me from a sound sleep.
- The results of inadequate sleep were plentiful. My energy level was low, as was my tolerance threshold. I found myself becoming irrationally frustrated by the slightest perceived misdeed. I was so tired after a long day at work that I was falling asleep on the couch when I should have been actively engaged with my children. I knew I had to make a change. And I did. It took some work, and the work

is far from over, but I'll certainly share how I went about getting the sleep I needed.
- I'd offer that one way you can increase your sleep time is by grabbing a calendar and penciling in set times that are available for work outside of school. These should be times that will not interfere with family time and will not stretch late into the night. Once you've established a schedule, stick to it! It's a helpful exercise and one that'll help you sleep soundly at night. Here's a look at the calendar I've created this past school year that has helped me get my sleep back on track (Note: This calendar represents profession related actions; it does not include family obligations):

Ryan's Work Schedule 2018-2019		
Day of the Week	In-School Work	After Hours Work
Sunday	N/A	Weekly Doctorate Work and Lesson Plan Review 8pm-10pm
Monday	School 7:45am-2:13pm Grading/Lesson Planning/Extra Help 2:13pm-4:30pm	Doctorate Work 8pm-10pm
Tuesday	School 7:45am-2:13pm	Weekly Podcast Work 2:35pm-4:30pm Doctorate Work 8pm-10pm
Wednesday	School 7:45am-2:13pm Extra Help 2:13pm-3:15pm Curriculum Coordinator Meeting 3:30pm-4:30pm	**OFF NIGHT** (Twitter Chats)
Thursday	School 7:45am-2:13pm	Podcast Final Editing and Doctoral Work 8pm-10:00pm
Friday	School 7:45am-2:15pm Gay-Straight Alliance 2:15pm-3:15pm	**OFF NIGHT**
Saturday	N/A	**OFF DAY**

Focus on Food and Exercise

- With our busy schedules, it can be challenging to ensure we're taking proper care of ourselves. We don't get a lot of time to eat during the school day. When we do, it's often

just enough time to gobble up the leftovers we managed to toss in a Tupperware container a few minutes before leaving the house. As a result, we can find ourselves leaving school and either heading to a fast-food joint or overindulging at home. I was guilty of doing just that myself. I soon found myself gaining considerable weight. My self-confidence took a nosedive, and I felt lethargic daily. It was challenging to be the teacher I needed to be for my students.
- Soon, I realized I needed to get myself together. I put on emphasis on eating better and exercising (I'm enjoying running, although my 5k time continues to be embarrassing). I can't say enough about how much it's improved the way I've felt, both physically and emotionally!

Use Your Sick Days

- When you're sick, you're sick. Call out and rest. You're doing no one any good by forcing yourself into school when you're ill. You won't be able to teach effectively and you'll put your students and colleagues at risk for catching whatever it is you're currently fighting off.
- I know it's hard to call-out and the guilt can weigh us down a bit. However, it's the right thing to do for you and your students. Take care of yourself! It's the only way you can be the teacher leader your kids need.

EMOTIONAL SELF-CARE

While it's crucial to maintain our physical self-care over a grueling school year, it's just as vital we take care of ourselves emotionally. While life will always throw us a curveball here and there, we can take proactive measures to ensure we're continually feeling emotionally recharged and ready for the challenges that await.

Put a Premium on Family Time

- Family first. There's nothing else that needs to be said.

Don't Let Go of Hobbies

- I know it's hard and you'll probably feel guilty in taking time to enjoy a hobby when you know there's something you could be doing related to the job. But we can't afford to cast away all the things that have continued to bring us great joy for so many years. It's always a soul-refreshing moment that reminds us of who we are and who we can be. The happiness that envelops us as we partake in these hobbies will carry over into the classroom.
- So the next time you're presented with an opportunity to take in a movie, a concert, or a play...take it! The next time you have the opportunity to pick up the guitar or sit at the piano for a couple of hours...take it! The next time you have the opportunity to get together with friends for dinner or a game night...take it! You won't regret it.
- If indulging in one of your favorite hobbies requires you to take a personal day, TAKE IT! That's what they are there for. Never feel guilty about taking your well-deserved personal days.

Don't Suppress Emotions

- This job will leave us feeling a myriad of emotions. At any given time, we may find ourselves feeling happy, frustrated, sad, etc. It's normal. Allow yourself time to sit with each emotion and reflect upon how certain interactions and events led to these feelings. Let yourself smile when overjoyed. Allow yourself tears to fall when sadness reigns.
- Do not suppress emotions, as bottling them up will only lead to an eventual explosion. Soon you'll find yourself

questioning your work. You'll find yourself feeling burnt out. Stay mindful of how you're feeling and why. Allow the emotions to help make necessary changes to help ensure you're not only an effective classroom educator; you're also a satisfied classroom educator.

SECTION FOUR

Deliver

DELIVER HIGH-QUALITY INSTRUCTION

IDENTIFY STUDENT LEARNING PREFERENCES

As I'm sure you're aware, there's a lot of talk within the education community regarding the various "learning styles" of students. You're likely to continue hearing about these styles throughout your tenure as an educator, particularly when it comes to lesson planning. The basic premise of learning styles – visual, aural, verbal, physical, logical, social, and solitary – revolves around the notion that individual students learn best when presented information in a way that best matches their personality. As such, educators tailor their lessons to best meet the needs of their students.

Sounds perfect, right?

The problem, however, is that education researchers are continuing to present evidence that suggests learning styles simply do not exist. Pashler, McDaniel, Rohrer, and Bjork (2008) found no evidence to indicate a student's ability to learn and subsequently retain information was substantially improved by one learning style over another. So while students may certainly prefer learning a topic by way of a particular method, how information is ultimately presented has no effect on their ability to master a target objective.

So how does this impact our job?

While learning styles may be a misguided buzzword in education, it doesn't mean we should ignore student learning preferences altogether. Instead, we should focus on providing a variety of options for students to learn the information and subsequently demonstrate their mastery of the standard. The reason is that the learning preference of an individual student is likely to vary from lesson to lesson. By offering a buffet of options (Posey, 2019), students can pick and choose their preferred method of acquiring knowledge and demonstrating their ability to transfer the learning to an assigned assessment.

By offering choices to all students, we avoid labeling the children. Furthermore, we acknowledge *the* fact that varying approaches to a particular subject or topic has a direct effect on how students will go about learning it. Below is an example of how I attempt to provide students with choice as it relates to demonstrating acquired knowledge.

PLAN, PLAN, AND...PLAN

Lesson planning is one of the most important parts of teaching pedagogy. A well-written lesson and unit plan act as a GPS that will ultimately help guide both you and your students to the desired learning outcomes. But, it isn't always easy, and there's still much to take into consideration when constructing your units.

Is my unit culturally relevant? Will students of all races, gender identities, socioeconomic status, etc. feel safe and welcomed inside the classroom with each lesson?

Recommended Resources for Culturally Relevant Pedagogy:

- "But That's Just Good Teaching! The Case for Culturally Relevant Pedagogy" Gloria Ladson-Billings (1995).
- "Toward a Theory of Culturally Relevant Pedagogy" Gloria Ladson-Billings (1995).

- *"Culturally Sustaining Pedagogies" Django Paris and H. Samy Alim (2017).*

Did I plan for differentiated instruction to ensure all students can access the material?

- *Recommended Resource for Differentiated Instruction:*
- *"The Differentiated Classroom: Responding to the Needs of All Learners" Carol Ann Tomlinson (2014).*

Did I plan to scaffold and frontload vocabulary for English Learners?

- *Recommended Resource for Teaching EL Students:*
- *"The Language-Rich Classroom: A Research-Based Framework for Teaching English Language Learners" Persida Himmele and William Himmele (2009).*

What enrichment activity will I have for students who not only completed the task earlier than their peers, but also demonstrated mastery of the topic?

- *Recommended Resource for Enrichment Activities:*
- *"Engaging and Challenging Gifted Students: Tips for Supporting Extraordinary Minds in Your Classroom" Jenny Grant Rankin (2016).*

I used to find lesson planning a bit overwhelming. I didn't know how exactly I should format it or what information should be included. Then I came across Understanding by Design (or UbD as the kids like to say). UbD is an exquisite way to develop your lessons and units in a way that helps us see the big picture. By utilizing the Understanding by Design method of curriculum planning, you're focusing on the desired outcomes and then working backward to help make sure you've taken everything into account to ensure that each child in your classroom is given every opportunity to master the standards covered within the unit.

So what's Understanding by Design all about?

I'm glad you asked! Let's take a look.

UNDERSTANDING BY DESIGN

In late 2017, the district that I was employed by announced their desire to have all departments begin the process of reflecting upon all units, identifying areas that could be improved upon, and rewriting each unit as an UbD. It was an ambitious plan and one that would undoubtedly ruffle some feathers within each school building. However, given the potential for the UbD to help increase both student achievement and engagement, it was a risk worth taking.

Based primarily off the work of Jay McTighe and Grant Wiggins, *Understanding by Design* offers a planning process and structure to guide curriculum, assessment, and instruction. Its two key ideas are contained in the title: 1) focus on teaching and assessing for understanding and learning transfer, and 2) design curriculum "backward" from those ends (2011). Furthermore, the two educational leaders at the forefront of Understanding by Design have identified seven vital precepts to the approach to curricula writing (McTighe & Wiggins, 2011):

1. Learning is enhanced when teachers think purposefully about curricular planning.
2. The UbD framework helps focus curriculum and teaching

on the development and deepening of student understanding and transfer of learning.
3. Understanding is revealed when students autonomously make sense of and transfer their learning through authentic performance.
4. Effective curriculum is planned backward from long-term, desired results through a three-stage design process (Desired Results, Evidence, and Learning Plan).
5. Teachers are coaches of understanding, not mere purveyors of content knowledge, skill, or activity. They focus on ensuring that learning happens, not just teaching; they check for successful meaning-making and transfer by the learner.
6. Regularly reviewing units and curriculum against design standards enhances curricular quality and effectiveness.
7. The UbD framework reflects a continual improvement approach to student achievement and teacher craft.

If you're thinking that Understanding by Design is of interest to you moving forward but aren't exactly sure how to begin, here is the latest UbD template that was designed, created, and shared by Grant Wiggins & Jay McTighe (2011):

SAMPLE UBD TEMPLATE

Stage 1 Desired Results		
ESTABLISHED GOALS <type here>	*Transfer*	
	Students will be able to independently use their learning to... <type here>	
	Meaning	
	UNDERSTANDINGS Students will understand that... <type here>	ESSENTIAL QUESTIONS <type here>
	Acquisition	
	Students will know... <type here>	Students will be skilled at... <type here>
Stage 2 - Evidence		
Evaluative Criteria	**Assessment Evidence**	
<type here>	PERFORMANCE TASK(S): <type here>	
<type here>	OTHER EVIDENCE: <type here>	
Stage 3 – Learning Plan		
<type here>	*Summary of Key Learning Events and Instruction*	

Be sure to visit jaymctighe.com for additional information and resources as it relates to Understanding by Design!

DELIVER MEANINGFUL FEEDBACK

CHANGE THE MINDSET

Grading will always be an oft-debated topic within the field of education. It's easy to see why. Grades mean a lot right now. The letter or number at the top of a page or inside a report card is what students and parents/guardians are accustomed to fixate on while schools use these marks for data collection, analysis, and, in some cases, teacher evaluations. But are we doing our students a disservice by focusing too much on the final grade rather than on the year-long journey toward improvement? I'd argue that we are.

DON'T WAIT UNTIL THE DUE DATE

One of the most common mistakes made by teachers, regardless of experience (myself included), is to fail to provide actionable feedback to students during an assignment. Rather, many teachers wait until returning the finished product to students with a grade along with some general comments. To be honest, it's not surprising that this type of feedback is happening due to time constraints, class sizes, and so on. However, we must make a concerted effort to move away from this practice as it is ultimately not in the best interest of student learning.

As mentioned earlier, students (and parents) are typically grade-centered when it comes to returned work. Kids especially are more likely to perseverate on the actual letter or number grade rather than examining the identified areas in need of improvement. It's not their fault. They've been conditioned to respond in such a way. It's up to us to get them out of that mindset and put the focus on where it truly belongs: the process and continual improvement.

CREATE A STRONG RUBRIC

I don't know about you, but I love a good rubric. They make grading a much more streamlined process. With a rubric, you're certainly going to significantly cut down on time you spend grading pieces of writing, projects, and presentations. However, it must be noted that in order to ensure that students are continually progressing toward mastery, the rubric must be standards-based with desired outcomes clearly defined. It is also essential to provide personalized feedback that points the student in the right direction. Simply put, a poorly executed rubric will make it impossible to ascertain a student's ability concerning the activity's target objective.

When I look back upon some of my old rubrics, I can't help but feel like I did students a disservice at times. While my intentions were good, the impact certainly wasn't what I hoped it would be for the kids. Because of how I formatted my rubrics, I wasn't always providing helpful feedback. There were times when I was giving points to a student for simple acts of compliance. *Oh, you put a heading on the paper?* Great. Here are five points. Why exactly was I putting acts of compliance on a rubric that was meant to ascertain a student's growth relative to the standards being assessed? I knew I needed to conduct research and find a better way to provide students with a better rubric.

One of my favorite styles of rubric is the **single-point rubric**. I first discovered this method of measuring student performance from Jennifer Gonzalez's site, *The Cult of Pedagogy*. I'm sure you've heard of it? Anyway, Gonzalez (2015) points out the single-point rubric's simplicity allows us to provide students with "higher-quality feedback." While the rubric itself is simplistic in design, it requires teachers to clearly identify areas of strengths as well as areas in need of improvement (Gonzalez, 2015). Here's a recent single-point rubric template offered by Gonzalez (2017) on *The Cult of Pedagogy* website:

Criteria (or Standard)	1	2	3	4	Feedback
Use this to describe different criteria. Then rate student work with one of the four numbers to the right.		✓			Can be used to explain number score, give suggestions for improvement, or for pushing even further.
			✓		
				✓	
			✓		

1 - standard not met, 2 - standard partially met, 3 - standard met, 4 - exceeds expectations

Additional Resources for Rubric Design:

- *How to Create and Use Rubrics for Formative Assessment and Grading* (2013) by Susan M. Brookhart
- Visit *Quality Rubrics Wiki Page* curated by Jennifer Binis (Twitter: @JennBinis) for extraordinary insight on rubric design.
- Link: http://qualityrubrics.pbworks.com

STUDENT CONFERENCES

I'm just going to put it all out there right now. Student conferences are one of my favorite parts of the job. Over the years, I've found that students respond amazingly well to praise and constructive criticism during 1-on-1 student-teacher conferences. For the most part, I use these meetings as an opportunity to critically review student writing. As I've said previously, I want students' mindsets to change. I do not want them focused solely on the grade. I want an opportunity to have an open and honest conversation as it relates to their year-long journey in my classroom. And you know what? So do they!

Mr. McHale's Argumentative Paper and the Feedback Loop: A Case Study

Each year, I assign my eighth grade English language arts students with the task of completing an argumentative paper. For this particular assignment, I allow students to pick a social justice issue, align with a side, and conduct extensive research on the topic to put their paper together. I try to push students to pick a topic on which their opinion has yet to be fully formed. While it is not my job to tell my students WHAT to think, I certainly must assist them in learning HOW to think. I want my students to dig deep into a topic that they may not know much about. I want them piecing together evidence from various sources, synthesizing the information, and formulating an opinion that they confidently stand by. It's a multi-step process and one that requires frequent checking-in to ensure students are making adequate gains daily. As such, I put together a feedback loop that would allow me to work alongside students throughout the project, providing them with helpful, non-evaluative critiques before turning in their finished product.

Step 1: Give Clear Instructions for Assignment and Provide an Exemplar

Early in my career, one of my most glaring weaknesses as a teacher was a lack of clarity when first introducing a large-scale writing assignment. As educators, we are used to writing paper after paper. Perhaps we forget just how chaotic the writing process can be. We forget how maddening it can be to narrow down and simplify our topic. We forget how there can be days when the words are just failing to formulate correctly on the page in front of us. On those days, it feels as though we are incapable of cohesively stringing together our thoughts. Now imagine feeling that way as a middle school student!

Over time, I realized that my expectations for written work were far too high. I would frequently become exasperated by the amount of time I spent evaluating papers. It wasn't that the kids were incapable of producing fantastic written products. They must certainly were.

But why weren't these papers meeting or exceeding expectations?

Sometimes we as educators are quick to pass the blame on to the children. I realized at that moment that it wasn't the kid's fault they were struggling mightily with the assignment. It was my fault. I was the problem.

Upon self-reflection, I realized that I wasn't clear in my expectations of what the final product should look like. I made terrible assumptions. To compound the issue, I failed to show my students an exemplar paper from a past student. Those were some bush-league errors on my part. Why should I have assumed they could produce a paper that met my rigorous expectations when I had neither clearly discussed how those expectations would manifest themselves within their papers, or showed them an example of an assignment done to near perfection?

Ever since I came to the realization that it was my inefficacy that was leading to frustration, I became determined to make things right. Today, I make it a point to spend as much time as needed to clearly outline each assignment and its expectations as well as produce at least one exemplar (either a student's work from a previous year or a self-created example) for students to review. The increased attention to the start of each new project has produced far greater student gains thus far.

Step 2: Write Alongside Your Students!

Providing students with an exemplar of the assignment you're currently asking them to complete is, without a doubt, a highly beneficial action. In doing so, you're providing each child with an opportunity to visualize how the final copy should appear. However, that offering may not be enough in itself to increase a student's level of confidence. There will almost certainly be an issue with confidence on the part of the student. Kids are typically nervous about any written assignment. The reason? The fear of making a mistake.

One way to combat their insecurities with writing is to write as well. Students absolutely love to see you working on the same assignment that they're currently attacking. It creates a sense of community within the classroom. Everyone is on the same page. Everyone on a mission.

The fact is that students want to know that they are not the only ones who struggle with writing. It's wonderfully reassuring to see an adult taking their time writing an essay, also struggling to find the right words and making grammatical errors along the way.

When I write an assignment that I've asked my students to complete, I will often project my Google Doc on to the classroom whiteboard as well as share it on Google Classroom to ensure that all students have access to my work as they proceed with the project. I want them to see how writing is not an inherently easy undertaking. Writing well takes time, practice, and patience. It's a grind. But once you're in a rhythm, it's one of the more enjoyable activities we can do.

Now, I know what you're thinking. How can we possibly write our own paper, check in with students, and provide actionable feedback? For starters, I'm not suggesting you necessarily write an entire paper. Write enough to help students understand the gist of what's expected and see your thought process. Typically, I write at least an introduction, one supporting paragraph with a transition to the next point, and a conclusion.

Step 3: Sit with a New Group of Students Each Day

In addition to writing your own paper in class, the next step in helping all your students out over the course of the assignment is to sit with a new group of students each day. After I speak with my students for the first 5-10 minutes of class (most likely displaying my work on the overhead projector), I disconnect my laptop from the projector cables, tuck the computer under my arm, and sit with a cluster of students.

I've noticed that when I sit with students, at their table and on their level, productivity increases. It starts to feel as though we're all on a mission together. We are all working on completing the task in front of us. I know that I tend to focus in on the assignment! While one may argue that sitting at a table with students may cause a fear-based form of compliance rather than a demonstration of understanding and transfer, if you've worked hard to create a collaborative and welcoming environment within your classroom that argument begins to crumble.

Throughout class, I'll not only be working on the assignment, but I'll be talking up the kids at the table. I'll see how their day is going and ask if they need clarification on directions or general expectations. After a bit of time, I'll take a look at the work of each student at my table and offer real-time, actionable feedback for them to reflect upon. In those moments, I see light bulbs go off. I'm noticing confidence levels increasing. I know that those three or four students at the table are leaving that day's class with specific teacher feedback. Of course, I'll be there to answer questions and assist all students throughout the class, but my mission for that day is to give as specific feedback as possible with the kids I'm sitting beside. I'll repeat the process throughout the assignment until I've had the opportunity to sit alongside all students in the class.

Step 4: Leverage Technology to Provide Actionable Feedback to Students

I'm certainly a fan of incorporating technology within the classroom setting. However, I believe that education consultants, Tom Murray and Eric Sheninger (2017), hit the nail on the head in their book, *Learning Transformed*, when they mention that technology is meant to be used as an accelerant to learning rather than be seen as a magic cure-all for student academic achievement. They go on to mention that the learning needs to be considered first and the technology second (Murray & Sheninger, 2017). They're right. Identify your learning outcomes first and then utilize available technological means to help accelerate the learning of said desired outcome.

I've personally found technology to be most helpful in the area of student writing. Thanks to Google Classroom, you can create an assignment using a Google Doc and step right in to documents that students are writing in to see how they're faring in real-time. In addition, you can leave a comment that'll pop up for the student to read. Personally, I will hop in each document once per class and do a quick look-through. I'll be sure to either make a suggestion or, in most cases, leave a note of encouragement. Regardless of the type of feedback left, I can take a look at the progress all students are e making. The kids know that although I may be sitting with a few kids, I have a firm grasp on the progress of the class as a whole. As much as kids enjoy my time at their table, they also know that I am always accessible and attending to their needs every day.

DELIVER CONSISTENT CLASSROOM MANAGEMENT

AH YES…SETTING THE TONE!

We talked a little bit ago about the importance of setting the right tone on the first day of school. I mentioned it once again because it's critically important to having a successful school year. Once the year starts flying, it is a challenging endeavor to improve the classroom atmosphere if the proper tone isn't set early on.

This emphasis on tone is not to suggest that it's drenched in superiority complex. It's not a power move. The tone does not have to be grounded in fear, nor should it be. Instead, our tone should be firm in that we are explicitly stating what we (teacher and students) are going to accomplish throughout our time together and what classroom expectations will need to be followed to achieve our goals.

CREATE A LIST OF NON-NEGOTIABLES

As the classroom teacher, you already have a sense of what needs to be taught, how you want to teach the material, and the classroom conditions that'll be required to ensure student learning. With that in mind, you should have a list of non-negotiables as it relates to behavioral expectations.

The list of non-negotiables that you announce to your students does not have to be dropped like Thor's hammer. The list is not meant to be seen as a threat for punishment. Instead, the non-negotiables should be presented as classroom norms that are in place to ensure that our students are afforded the opportunity to learn while feeling safe and welcomed within the confines of the room.

While lists of classroom non-negotiable rules may vary from teacher to teacher, here are a few successful ones that I've used, seen, or heard:

- All students are to be respected at all times.
- Please refrain from distracting others.
- Keep hands and feet to yourself.
- There's no place for hateful words and actions in this room.
- Be mindful and present during class.

ALLOW STUDENTS TO VOICE OPINIONS

The list of non-negotiables will certainly not be a complete list of the classroom room norms that'll be necessary to ensure learning. It's here that I like to add in student voice. From a purely anecdotal standpoint, I'm of the mind that all students want to do well. They want to be put in the best positive to succeed. As a result, you'll likely be thrilled by the spirited discussion that will take place when you open the floor to student suggestions.

By allowing students to help in the formation of classroom expectations, you're allowing kids to see the big picture. They understand that the job in front of them will require dedication and perseverance to be successful. As such, they will be willing to hold themselves accountable. In many previous classes, it has been the students who argued for no cell phones, immediate parent phone calls for misbehavior or poor academic performance, and even an agreement that extra credit shouldn't exist if one failed to complete previously assigned work.

While many classrooms across the country have such rules in place from day one, too many were established by the adult in a way that assumed students didn't know any better. However, the kids are alright. If given a chance, they'll show you that they can be successful and even blow past any expectation that we as educators may have had. Also, when kids are helping to establish a set of classroom norms, they are much more willing to engage in dialogue and accept the consequences, should they disregard the rules they helped put into place.

MUTUALLY AGREE UPON CONSEQUENCES

Ok, honest talk. Consequences will always be a part of teaching. There's just no other way around it. Saying anything else would be downright disingenuous. We are, after all, working daily with incredibly young children who are still learning and growing. Mistakes will happen. However, how you decide to go about consequencing a child can have a tremendous impact on how they feel about your class and school in general. There's a way to hold students accountable in a manner that will allow you to issue discipline in a way that preserves your relationship with the child.

THE SEATING CONUNDRUM

Regardless of where you are on your journey in education, the issue of classroom design and seating arrangement will always be rattling in your mind. We will forever be pondering the effectiveness of seating as it relates to student academic achievement and social growth, as we should! That said, you'll often hear two terms repeated endlessly when it comes to grouping your students: flexible seating and assigned seating. For some, it's an all or nothing proposition. You're either all-in with flexible seating, or you're content with assigning your students a specific place within the confines of your classroom. I respectfully disagree with this notion. For me, it's all about understanding your students and their academic and social needs and then acting accordingly.

Flexible Seating vs. Seating Charts

Flexible seating is all the rage these days. All the kids are talking about it. In essence, flexible seating is an open classroom concept. Desks are not arranged in rows. In fact, there may be minimal desks in the room to begin with. There may be a couch in one corner or a row of standing desks in the back of the room. You may find bean bag chairs and a reading nook over in another corner. The goal is to create a relaxed and welcoming environment, one in which students look forward to entering and leave behind their outside troubles for a class period. Sounds amazing, right?

I agree that the concept of flexible seating is fascinating and worthy of consideration when planning your room setup. However, there are still benefits to a standard classroom setup where desks may be grouped together or in rows with the purpose of assigned students a specific seat. It doesn't have to be the malicious attempt to demonstrate one's power over today's youth as others may lead you to believe. There are many reasons why assigned seating may be highly beneficial for the purposes of your class.

Should I ever feel compelled to provide a student with an assigned seat, I'm never doing so as a punishment. There are so many factors that go into making such a decision, and I make sure to clearly reflect on the reasons for creating a seating chart.

Regardless of whether you're intent on flexible seating or sticking with the time-tested seating chart, I would recommend starting out the year with assigned spots within the classroom. It's essential to focus on learning the names of students, building a relationship with each child, and installing a concrete set of classroom expectations. Once those three tasks have been checked off the to-do list, you'll feel comfortable in going with the seating arrangement that best meets the needs of your students.

STICK TO IT!

No matter what rules you establish for your classroom, chaos will eventually reign if you fail to be consistent in following through with your management plan. It's quite simple, really. When students do something inappropriate or against school rules and go without a consequence, they're more likely to continue test boundaries in an attempt to see how much they can get away with. And let's be honest…that's not a student issue. That's a human issue. We're all guilty of, at one time or another, pushing the envelope if we feel it's safe to do so.

As a result, it's vital that consequences are issued once you establish your set of non-negotiables in addition to the classroom norms that were created in collaboration with your students. Students will know where the line has been drawn, and they'll also be more receptive to discussing an issue since the conversation has become transparent and clear-cut. You can now calmly explain that an infraction warrants a consequence as was discussed and agreed upon in the very first days of school. There's no need for a back and forth argument because you've already identified the location of "the line," and you're now addressing the action as soon as it crosses that mutually agreed-upon threshold. So what are some typically effective non-negotiable rules for the classroom? For me, I only had two:

1. Respect everyone in the room (including yourself).
2. Actively listen to one another.

That's it. All those other commonly found rules of today's classroom? You know the rules about gum, cell phones, cheating, and all that? I ultimately found that those were the rules that students would come up with on their own when I asked them to help me create class norms. By allowing myself to be vulnerable and relinquish some control, I provided kids with an opportunity to recognize what needs to be done to achieve success. They did not have to be yelled at or threatened with severe consequences. They just needed a chance to see it for themselves. That's all they've ever needed.

And as for consequences? I put a lot of effort into rectifying a situation within my own sphere of influence without sending a child out of the classroom and to the office. Here are the typical consequences I'd put in place within the classroom:

A quick and subtle check-in with the student.

- Kneel beside the desk and ask if everything's ok. Ask the student to refocus or, if necessary, take a mental break for a moment before returning to work.

Ask the student to stay behind after class.

- Allow the class to exit the room and briefly chat with a student who may have had a difficult time adhering to class norms. Clearly communicate that you care about them and could tell something was on their mind today. Inquire about what may be going on and ask the child to reflect upon the class. Was there anything they could have done differently? More importantly, was there anything that I could have done differently to help ensure they had a better class experience?

Call home.

- After all these years, I still find calling a parent or guardian to discuss any incident from class to be one of the most highly effective ways of helping improve academic and social performance within the classroom. It takes little time, and if you frame the conversation in a way that conveys concern rather than anger, you'll likely get full support from home.

Detention.

- Detention is my least favorite consequence to issue. However, sometimes an action will necessitate doling out a detention slip. In those cases, I try to ensure that the detention is meaningful. I honestly don't want a silent detention in which a young child sits alone, forced to do homework. I want a conversation. I want to engage in meaningful dialogue and see if I can understand what's troubling my student. Is there anything I can do? Is there someone else that I can refer them to?
- Furthermore, I always hold detention after school and never during lunch. Students, regardless of what they may have done to earn a teacher detention, need that time to regroup and be with friends. I have a tough time believing that taking that time away from them will do anything to positively impact future behavior.

While I did not include sending a child to the office or any other harsher punishments commonly found in school on this list, that's not to say there aren't actions that require a more significant consequence. Obviously, incidents involving bullying, sexual misconduct, violence, and drug use will need to be handled by your administrative team. I am, however, suggesting that we reflect upon the steps we take when the time eventually comes that requires us to discuss classroom protocol with students. We don't need to issue detentions and/or office referrals for every little perceived slight. And for the love of everything...just give the student a pencil!

DELIVER CONTINUOUS SOCIAL-EMOTIONAL SUPPORT
Help Strengthen a Growth Mindset

In 2006, a Professor of Psychology at Stanford University published a groundbreaking text called *Mindset: The New Psychology of Success*. Carol Dweck, the author of the aforementioned text, defined two distinct types of mindset present in human beings: the fixed mindset and the growth mindset. In *Mindset*, Dweck provided readers with the following definitions of the two trains of thought:

Fixed Mindset: A fixed mindset is a belief that we're born with a set amount of intelligence and ability. It's difficult to achieve an optimal amount of academic and social success while operating with a fixed mindset. People operating in the fixed mindset are prone to avoiding challenges and failures, thereby robbing themselves of a life rich in experience and learning (Dweck, 2006, p.24).

Growth Mindset: The belief that with practice, perseverance, and effort, people have limitless potential to learn and grow. People operating in the growth mindset tackle challenges with aplomb, unconcerned with making mistakes or being embarrassed, focusing instead on the process of growth (Dweck, 2006, p.30).

It's becoming increasingly important for today's educators to focus on ingraining growth mindset within their students' psyche. As I reflect upon my first ten years in education, I'm noticing that children these days appear more apt to run away from a challenge, preferring instead to wave the white flag in defeat rather than pushing through the perceived immovable obstacle standing in front of them.

THE PROBLEM WITH FIXED MINDSET

The fixed mindset, especially in young children, can be the ultimate detriment in a student's quest to achieve optimal levels of academic and social growth within a given school year. When a child begins questioning their own ability to learn, retain, and apply new information, they quickly become apathetic. These students will feel no reason to put forth their best effort in class and on assessments. To them, it's an exercise in futility. If, in their mind, they are incapable of performing at a level higher than they've achieved in the past, why waste additional time prepping for the same result?

A fixed mindset will make progress virtually impossible. After all, the goal of every lesson is to provide each student with the knowledge necessary to build upon a previously acquired skill. A student with a fixed mindset, unfortunately, will tend to believe that they're destined to only reach a certain point before their brain comes to a screeching halt.

A GROWTH MINDSET CAN PROPEL STUDENTS

Whereas students with a fixed mindset tend to fasten themselves to a contrived world of mediocrity, kids with a firm growth mindset believe the sky's the limit. They are willing to take risks to find success. They're able to accept constructive criticism, knowing the information passed along is given with the best of intentions. Students with a growth mindset understand that to ultimately win the game called life, they must accept that there will be losses along the way.

While teachers may get frustrated with students with a fixed mindset, they mustn't give up on those kids. The good news is that a growth mindset can be taught. Will it be easy? Absolutely not. It's hard to change a person's perception of themselves. However, it can be done.

HOW TO FOSTER GROWTH MINDSET

There are dozens of ways a teacher can ultimately help a student develop a growth mindset. I firmly believe that the individual teacher should have the autonomy to use the methods that work best for them. However, if you're trying to put together a list together and could use a few suggestions, here are some techniques you may consider.

- **Ditch the Word "Failed."**

Instead, focus on the term "learning opportunity." The student may have under-performed the first time. However, they shouldn't be allowed to think that they can't ultimately achieve success with the assessed material. Help them see that, whether or not they're afforded the opportunity to try the exam again, the grade doesn't define their ultimate ability. The grade simply defined their understanding of standards at a given point in time. With a willingness to put forth effort and risk stumbling on the journey to knowledge, students will begin to see that their success in the classroom has not been predetermined.

- **Share a Personal Anecdote**

I've never prescribed to the notion that a teacher must be a robotic, soulless version of the person they are outside of school. Over the years, I've found that students want to develop a genuine connection with their educators. They want to establish a sense of comfort within the four walls of their classroom. That's a good thing. Their comfort with you will allow them to ask that lingering question, attend after-school extra help sessions, and strive to make you proud of their accomplishments. Don't be afraid to open up and be human in front of your students.

We didn't get to where we are now by being perfect every second of every day since birth. We've made our fair share of mistakes and miscalculations. But, we learned from them. We grew from them. Ultimately, we found success from them. Let your students know that. Give them concrete examples of how you once overcame what seemed, at the time, to be insurmountable odds. Let them know that if you were able to make the necessary adjustments to succeed, they can too.

- **Promote Grit...But Only to an Extent**

> *Grit (noun): passion and perseverance for long-term goals (Duckworth, 2016).*

Grit is a word that has recently started being shouted from the rooftop of every school across the country. Yes, it's a powerful tool. In fact, Angela Duckworth, author of *Grit: The Power of Passion and Perseverance*, tells us it's a person's grit, not IQ, that may be the most instrumental determiner of future success. In the New York Times Bestseller, Duckworth (2016) tells of her own personal epiphany as she became determined to find success through grit. "I'll challenge myself every day. When I get knocked down, I'll get back up. I may not be the smartest person in the room, but I'll strive to be the grittiest").

We need to do our part to help cultivate a future generation comprised of global citizens who will fight for their goals, who will take calculated risks to achieve success, and will see disappointing results as an opportunity to better themselves. We, as educators, have the ability to have a profound impact on the future. By promoting grit, we are helping students prepare for the challenges that'll inevitably come their way.

While grit is, without a doubt, a beneficial character trait, we must not forget that a critical component of grit is passion. Without the desire to push through difficult times, we cannot reasonably expect a child to display grit. We must not forget that in order for a child to pick themselves up after they've stumbled, they must be able to see the benefits to such an arduous journey. It is here where we have to be cognizant of the need to help students understand the real-world benefits to each and every lesson and assignment. If we are simply going through the motions or outwardly appear disinterested in the topic we're presenting, it's wholly unfair to hold students accountable to any perceived lack of grit.

We must also understand that for many of our students, particularly students of color who have been forced to continually pick themselves up after being knocked down by a country steeped in systemic racism, grit is already a part of who they are. Author Bettina L. Love (2019) eloquently explains this truth in her remarkable book, *We Want to Do More Than Survive*. She states that African Americans, for years upon years, have had to have grit simply to survive in the United States. As such, grit has been ingrained within the DNA of Black children. To constantly push the notion of grit upon Black students is, as Love (2019) notes, like pushing the "Beating the Odds" narrative typically found in literature, film, and television.

Love makes a gut-wrenching point here that should resonate among educators. The education system, as designed, tends to see the academic and social success of students of color as a miracle worth celebrating. Rather than tackling the sources of inequity within the field, we are metaphorically throwing a parade in honor of non-white students for essentially beating the system. Love (2019) goes on to inform readers of an award issued by the Governor's Office of Student Achievement in Georgia and imparted upon schools that "beat the odds." She notes that the award is calculated by "comparing schools' ability to teach based on student characteristics that are 'outside the school's control such as race, ethnicity, disabilities, English fluency, economic 'disadvantage' and transience" (p. 73). The troubling fact, as Love (2019) notes, is that only 40% of schools in Georgia so-called "beat the odds."

Grit isn't the problem. The system is the problem. Georgia, like I'm sure many other states across the country do, celebrate the seemingly surprising success of non-white students rather than tackling the crippling systemic racism, sexism, and ableism that oppresses the same children. A child's perceived level of grit related to their academic and social performance should never be questioned. For many of the children in front of us daily, grit has already been instilled upon them due to having to overcome the inequities that exist across all aspects of life in America. It's not a matter of measuring the amount of grit within a child. It's a matter of whether or not we, as educators, are doing enough within a given lesson to activate that grit to ensure each child is able to work through the struggles of learning. The question that we should have on the forefront of our mind when thinking of grit is, "Are we presenting the lesson in a manner that is engaging and relatable so that our students are activating their grit to master the topic at hand?"

BELIEVE THAT GROWTH OF MIND WILL LEAD TO GROWTH IN ACHIEVEMENT

The entire premise of cultivating a student body with a growth mindset is predicated on the belief that a school's faculty will be on board with the culture shift. While it'll be difficult to see immediate results by the fostering of growth mindset, trust the theory. Over time, the fruit of your labor will become clear.

LOVE IS AN OPEN DOOR

One of the phrases that I'm constantly saying to kids and parents is that I have an open-door policy. While I am contractually obligated to set aside a one-hour block per week as an after school extra help session, I repeatedly tell students and families that if I'm in the building, I'm available to provide academic and social support. Whether it's allowing a couple of kids to sit in my classroom at lunch because they're having a rough day or working around a parent's work schedule to provide a child with extra help, I'm always more than happy to accommodate students to ensure they feel safe and supported within the confines of the building.

Realistically, you more than likely won't have many students taking you up on the offer to come in during non-office hours. However, it's the offer that makes the difference. For that student and their family, knowing that you're willing to offer your time to meet their needs creates a sense of trust that is necessary to thrive with rigorous academic and social expectations.

Mr. McHale's Spoken Word Poetry Club: A Case Study

My first year as an eighth-grade teacher was an eye-opening experience. I had previously taught 6th grade ELA for many years, but I yearned for an opportunity to read, analyze, and discuss higher-level works of literature. I was floored after just the first week of classes. I couldn't believe how much more mature these 8th graders were compared to when I last worked with many of them only two years prior. They were beginning to articulate their world views. They were navigating the craziness of teenage life at a time when hormones were raging. They questioned authority and debated the purposefulness of certain school norms. Honestly, as an educator, it was reinvigorating.

But I knew that with such rapid changes, both mentally and physically, many of the kids in front of me were left feeling confused and alone. I hadn't honestly noticed until I reached the poetry unit of my ELA curriculum.

I knew going into that school year that I wanted to overhaul the eighth-grade poetry unit. I desired to find a way to get young kids to see the beauty in poetry. While the poets typically found in the standard (see: White) literary canon produced well-written forms of prose, the reality remained that today's youth would often struggle to connect with the "classics." And then I found spoken-word poetry.

Spoken word poetry, commonly referred to as performance poetry, is an in-your-face, "here are my feelings" type of poem. These emotionally captivating forms of poetry often tackled complicated subject matter that allowed the poet an opportunity to release the inner thoughts that once felt trapped inside. The performances of these poems (and you can check out a litany of videos through Button Poetry's YouTube Channel) would leave students awe-struck. The more we discussed spoken word, watched performances, and wrote our own pieces, the more kids wanted to keep the unit going.

Unfortunately, time is never on our side as educators. At some point, we will have to move on from one unit to ensure we have plenty of time for the next. However, I saw that, for some of my students, the spoken word poetry unit was somewhat of a life-altering experience. They saw spoken word as an outlet; an opportunity to unleash the mishmash of anger, confusion, and joy that coursed through their minds daily. I wanted desperately to provide them with time to connect with other like-minded students to continue researching, writing, and performing pieces of poetry.

DELIVER ON PROMISES

Throughout this book, we've discussed the many ways in which you can become an effective teacher leader within your building. I'm sure you even think that there's too much to be done to reach such a level. Remember that being a leader isn't about completing each and every action floating around the pages of this book. Take your time and ease into your new role and gently incorporate ideas as confidence and comfortability grow. However, if you're looking for one way to be that leader for your students and peers right now, I've saved the best for last. Do you strive to be the teacher your students deserve? That your school, district, and community deserves? It starts by delivering on promises.

As a classroom teacher, you are setting the tone for students, parents, and the school in more ways than one. It goes beyond just what you say. It's also about what you do. It's as the saying goes, "Your actions speak louder than words." Throughout the school year, you'll tell students and families what they can expect from you as the teacher. I'm sure you'll agree to take on responsibilities doled out by your administrative team as well. The easiest way to solidify yourself as a leader is to simply deliver on the promises you've agreed upon.

Examples of promises we often make over the course of a given school year include:

STUDENT VOICE OPPORTUNITIES

Recently, student voice and choice have been widely discussed by classroom teachers. Educators have started to notice that student engagement levels have increased dramatically when the kids were allowed to have a say in such things as assessment options or book choices. It makes sense. The collective voice of students has historically been stifled by teachers and school administrators, and one has to wonder if the silencing of student voice has contributed to the issues such as non-compliance and apathy.

I've noticed that when students entrusted with the responsibility of charting a path to success within a given unit, they are more likely to be motivated to complete the task. From a student perspective, it must be nice to be a part of a class in which the teacher is authentically vulnerable to the point of openly displaying a willingness to cede control in the room.

Ultimately, the key to future success after promising students a plethora of opportunities to have their voice heard is to deliver on that pledge. Why is it so important? When you are promising students a chance to have their voices heard, they'll be excited. They'll perhaps view you as a different kind of teacher, one who notices that the kids have a lot to bring to the table. However, if the number of opportunities to offer students a chance to voice their opinions and/or concerns dwindles months into the school year, it could negatively impact their mindset heading into your class. If you do have to back off on student voice for a valid reason, be sure to communicate to the kids exactly why the old way of doing things is no longer on the table. Students desire (and deserve) to understand the reasoning for sudden changes and doing so can help you ensure that the vibe of your classes produces favorable conditions for learning.

GRADING

Grading practices in education are seemingly always under intense scrutiny. As a professional teacher, you are certainly afforded the opportunity to decide for yourself how your students should be assessed. You determine the weight of each assignment, of each category (homework, tests, presentations, etc.). As you begin to create your class syllabus, you'll want to carefully consider your grading policies. Once you have solidified your grading practice, be sure to clearly communicate said policies with students and families.

We must remain consistent in our grading practice and, if there are any changes to be made, have a firm grasp on your "why." Discuss your reasoning with students and families so that everyone understands the changes in expectations. I've seen so many of my students thrive when I've laid everything out in advance when I've shown them exactly what I'm hoping for with an assignment. Likewise, when I've failed to deliver clarity and consistency related to grading, it caused a significant increase in anxiety and, quite frankly, a well-deserved dose of pushback.

CLASSROOM MANAGEMENT

As previously noted, our classroom management sets the tone for our classes. We spend a considerable amount of time at the beginning of the school year hashing out our academic and behavioral expectations. The goal, at that time, is to proactively create a safe and welcoming space for all students that provides all children with an opportunity to thrive. Once we've done just that, we must stick to the plan.

Consider this for a moment. You've worked alongside your students to help understand each other and the overarching goals we have for the class. Everyone is in agreement and feeling great about the promises of a successful school year. Then, all of a sudden, you issued a consequence to a student for an infraction that goes well beyond the previously agreed upon management system. What would happen to the trust that you've been working on establishing with the kids in front of you? If you've agreed to it, stick to it.

CREATING A SAFE AND WELCOMING ENVIRONMENT FOR LGBTQIA STUDENTS

I want to wrap things up with a few words on the importance of creating and maintaining a positive school climate and culture for our LGBTQIA kids. We've talked at length about providing all students with an opportunity to thrive both academically and socially. The most effective way to ensure that happens is to ensure that the school environment is a safe and welcoming space for each and every child that steps foot through the front door. We previously spoke about the importance of being an anti-racist educator to help provide students of color with an equitable educational experience. It's also vital that we work just as tirelessly to provide another set of marginalized students with a chance to shine by upholding our promise to fortify our schools against discriminatory practices and unsafe learning conditions.

LGBTQIA+ Students

While there has been tremendous progress over the years as it relates to the rights of LGBTQIA individuals, recent governmental decisions such as the enactment of a policy that bans transgender citizens from serving in our armed forces along with attempts to allow for businesses to legally discriminate individuals based on sexual orientation (National Center for Transgender Equality, 2019), have threatened to undo all headway.

The not-so-subtle attempts by our government to strip citizens of their rights simply due to sexual orientation have sadly impacted the safety and sense of inclusion for our LGBTQIA students. GLSEN (Gay, Lesbian, and Straight Education Network) had documented evidence that the school landscape was improving and becoming much more inclusive for LGBTQIA kids. Unfortunately, the past couple of years have seen numbers level off, and progress has seemingly come to a halt. Consider these gut-wrenching statistics from the latest GLSEN School Climate Survey (2017):

- 34.8% of LGBTQIA students missed at least one day of school within the past month because they felt safe or uncomfortable.
- 40% of students intentionally avoided gender-segregated areas within school (bathrooms, locker rooms, etc.) out of fear for their safety.
- 56.6% of students reported hearing homophobic remarks from their teachers or other staff members.
- 98.5% of students reported hearing peers use "gay" in a negative manner.
- 62.2% of students reported being subjected to discriminatory school policies such as being prevented from bringing a same-sex partner to a school dance, barred from starting a Gay-Straight Alliance, or prohibited from writing about LGBTQIA topics for assignments.

We have to do better for our LGBTQIA students. It's simple as that. Be an ally for these tremendously brave students. Proudly proclaim your classroom as being a safe space! Are you ready to be an ally for our LGBTQIA students? Get started with ease by heading over to GLSEN.org and download their FREE Safe Space Kit. You'll be able to download a tremendous poster that can be displayed on your door designating your room as a place in which all students are welcomed.

The fact is that by jumping into this wonderfully hectic, yet incredibly rewarding, profession, we are making a promise to ourselves, our students, our colleagues, our building, and our school community to be the best educator we can be for each and every single child that walks through the doors. I humbly ask that you remember the importance of upholding these promises and work tirelessly to create a welcoming space for all children so you may assist in eradicating racism, sexism, and ableism from our schools. These are promises that simply must be kept.

EXIT TICKET

Congratulations, once again, on jumping into this worthwhile profession. As you've read, this job has its fair share of ups and downs. There will be days that you'll thank your lucky stars for the opportunity to help shape the lives of countless children. There will also be days where, in the midst of an emotional breakdown, you'll wonder if the job is worth the hassle. I believe that it is and I hope you do as well.

Please don't wait to find the right moment to take chances and disrupt the status quo. We've been doing the same things year in and year out for decades, and we continue to leave too many students, specifically our more marginalized students, behind. You have been hired in your current role because it was firmly believed that you would be a game-changer. So what are you waiting for? Be that game changer!

You can be a leader right out of the gate! Yes, it'll take time and energy. You'll have to immerse yourself in all aspects of the job. But I'll tell you what. You'll never feel like you've left anything on the table. You will know that you're giving your students and their families everything you got — day in and day out. No exceptions. L.E.A.D!

EXIT TICKET

Learn
Engage
Avoid
Deliver

Put it all together, and you'll be the educator that your students deserve.

So, what's next? The work! I hope you're excited to get rolling on this journey. To help you unpack all that we've talked about throughout this book, be sure to download a copy of the LEAD from Day One Educator's Journal. You'll find guiding questions designed to assist you throughout this coming school year and beyond. I wish you all the best as you continue in your career in education. Always remember that you're here for a reason. Never forget your 'WHY.' Be the leader that your students need you to be.

REFERENCES

Berg, J. H. (2018). *Leading in sync: Teacher leaders and principals working together for student learning.* Alexandria, VA, USA: ASCD.

Brinson, D., & Steiner, L. (2007). Building collective efficacy. *The Center for Comprehensive School Reform and Improvement.* Washington, DC, USA.

Brown, B. (2018). *Dare to lead: Brave work. Tough conversations. Whole hearts.* New York: Random House.

Brown v. Board of Education of Topeka, Implementation Decree; May 31, 1955; Records of the Supreme Court of the United States; Record Group 267; National Archives.

REFERENCES

Cantor, D. (2018, September 25). America's achievement gap — Made, not born? What a study of 30,000 students reveals about lowered expectations and poorer-quality instruction for kids of Color [Blog Post]. Retrieved from https://www.the74million.org/article/study-achievement-gap-not-inevitable-it-reflects-lower-expectations-poorer-quality-instruction-for-students-of-color/

Dahl, R. (2005). *Charlie and the chocolate factory*. London: Puffin.

DiAngelo, R. J. (2018). *White fragility: Why it's so hard for white people to talk about racism*. Boston: Beacon Press.

Duckworth, A. (2016). *Grit: The power of passion and perseverance* (First Scribner hardcover edition). New York: Scribner.

Dweck, C. S. (2006). *Mindset: The new psychology of success* (1st ed.). New York: Random House.

Ellwood, T. (2018, March 12). Toxic positivity: Why being positive isn't always enough to make your business successful. Retrieved from https://medium.com/@TaylorEllwood/toxic-positivity-why-being-positive-isnt-always-enough-to-make-your-business-successful-165d2261ccb2

GLSEN. 2017 National SchoolClimate Survey.

Retrieved from https://www.glsen.org/article/2017-national-school-climate-survey

Gonzalez, J. (2015, February 4). Meet the #singlepointrubric [Blog Post]. Retrieved from https://www.cultofpedagogy.com/single-point-rubric/

Harvard, B. (2018, July 12). Out of cite, Out of mind [Blog Post]. Retrieved from https://theeffortfuleducator.com/2018/07/12/out-of-cite-out-of-mind/

Hattie, J. (2018). 252 influences and effect sizes related to student achievement. Visible Learning. Retrieved from www.visiblelearningplus.com/content/250-influences-student-achievement

Illinois State Board of Education. (2018). Illinois social/emotional development standards of the Illinois early learning standards. Retrieved from https://www.isbe.net/pages/social-emotional-learning-standards.aspx

Kendall, F. E. (2002). *Understanding white privilege: Creating pathways to authentic relationships across race*. New York: Routledge.

Levenson, M. R. (2014). *Pathways to teacher leadership: Emerging models, changing roles*. Cambridge, MA: Harvard Education Press.

Love, B. L. (2019). *We want to do more than survive: abolitionist teaching and the pursuit of educational freedom.* Boston, MA: Beacon Press.

McIntosh, P. (1988). *White privilege and male privilege: A personal account of coming to see correspondences through work in women's studies.* Wellesley, MA: Wellesley College, Center for Research on Women.

National Center for Transgender Equality (2019). Retrieved from https://transequality.org/the-discrimination-administration

National Governors Association Center for Best Practices, Council of Chief State School Officers Title: Common Core State Standards Publisher: National Governors Association Center for Best Practices, Council of Chief State School Officers, Washington D.C. Copyright Date: 2010

Nolan, C. (2008) *The dark knight* [Motion Picture]. United States: Warner Bros. Pictures

Pashler, H., McDaniel, M., Rohrer, D., & Bjork, R. (2008). Learning styles: Concepts and evidence. *Psychological Science in the Public Interest, 9* (3), 105–119. https://doi.org/10.1111/j.1539-6053.2009.01038.x

Platitude. (2019). Oxford dictionaries. Retrieved

from https://en.oxforddictionaries.com/definition/platitude.

Plessy vs. Ferguson, Judgement, Decided May 18, 1896; Records of the Supreme Court of the United States; Record Group 267; *Plessy v. Ferguson*, 163, #15248, National Archives.

Posey, A. (2019). *Engage the brain: How to design for learning that taps into the power of emotion.* Alexandria, VA, USA: ASCD.

Racial Segregation. (2019). Encyclopedia Britannica. Retrieved from https://www.britannica.com/topic/racial-segregation

Riddle, T., & Sinclair, S. (2019). Racial disparities in school-based disciplinary actions are associated with county-level rates of racial bias. *Proceedings of the National Academy of Sciences*, *116*(17), 8255. https://doi.org/10.1073/pnas.1808307116

Ronfeldt, M., Farmer, S. O., McQueen, K., & Grissom, J. A. (2015). Teacher collaboration in instructional teams and student achievement. *American Educational Research Journal*, *52*(3), 475–514. https://doi.org/10.3102/0002831215585562

Scott, M. (2018, March 25). *How to R.E.A.C.H.* Speech presented at ASCD Empower18 in Boston Convention and Exhibition Center, Boston, MA.

Sheninger, E. C., & Murray, T. C. (2017). *Learning transformed: 8 keys to designing tomorrow's schools, today*. Alexandria, VA: ASCD.

Style, E. (1988). Curriculum as window and mirror. Social Science Record, Fall, 1996. First published in Listening for All Voices, Oak Knoll School monograph, Summit, NJ, 1988. Retrieved from http://www.nationalseedproject.org/images/documents/Curriculum_As_Window_and_Mirror.pdf

Thomas, A. (2017). *The hate u give* (First edition). New York, NY: Balzer + Bray, an imprint of HarperCollinsPublishers.

U.S. Const. amend. XIV

U.S. Department of Education Office of Civil Rights. (2014, March 21). Civil rights data collection: Data snapshot (College and Career Readiness). Retrieved from https://www2.ed.gov/about/offices/list/ocr/docs/crdc-college-and-career-readiness-snapshot.pdf

United States Department of Education. (2016). *The State of Racial Diversity in the Educator Workforce*. 42.

Wiggins, G. P., & McTighe, J. (2011). *The understanding by design guide to creating high-quality units*. Alexandria, Va.: ASCD.

REFERENCES

Wilder, G., Albertson, J., Stuart, M., Dahl, R., & Warner Home Video (Film). (2011). *Willy Wonka & the chocolate factory*. United States: Warner Home Video.

Wright, A. (2015). Teachers' perceptions of students' behavior: The effect of racial congruence and consequences for school suspension. University of California, Santa Barbara. Retrieved from https://aefpweb.org/sites/default/files/webform/41/Race%20Match,%20Disruptive%20Behavior,%20and%20School%20Suspension.pdf

ABOUT THE AUTHOR

Ryan McHale is currently in his 10th year working as an English Language Arts teacher in Milford, Massachusetts. He is presently working alongside 8th graders in hopes of helping them become academically and socially prepared for the challenges that await them in high school. In addition to fulfilling his role as an anti-bias classroom teacher, Ryan serves as his building's Curriculum Coordinator, sits on the GLSEN-Massachusetts Board of Directors, and is actively working to earn his Doctoral Degree in Educational Leadership from the University of New England.

Ryan's goal with his book and podcast, Pondering Education, is two-fold. He desires to use his platform to not only help remind us all why we entered into the field of education, but to help pass along best practices from experts all around the country as well.

What you won't find from Ryan is overly negative commentary. While constructive criticism is both helpful and necessary at times, we all know that this job isn't an easy one. The last thing you need is to be reminded of the multitude of those roadblocks we encounter throughout a given school year. Instead, let's accentuate the positive! Let's work collaboratively to strengthen that intrinsic motivation that exists within all of us.

On a personal note, Ryan lives in Massachusetts with his wife and two young children. Mr. McHale absolutely loves living in the same area as his students as it's helped forge tremendous relationships with families all across town. In his spare time, you'll find Ryan taking in a concert from bands such as Phish, Dead and Company, Dave Matthews Band, and Pearl Jam.

facebook.com/ponderingeducation

twitter.com/PonderEducation

instagram.com/pondering_education

LEAD FROM DAY ONE
Educator Journal

Please feel free to write in answers to the following questions to help guide you in your journey toward becoming a teacher leader.

These questions can also be the basis for discussions on social media chats and Professional Learning events!

- What's your WHY? Why did you decide that teaching was the career for you? This is an answer that'll help center you when times get tough.

_____
_____
_____
_____
_____
_____
_____
_____
_____

- If your district is planning to provide (or has provided) a tour of the neighborhood prior to the start of school, what do you hope to have gained from the experience? If your district did not provide such a tour, what can you do to learn more about the community you serve?

- What is your school's mission statement?

- How will you work to ensure you're holding yourself accountable to uphold the mission statement?

- Identify one goal located in your district's long-term plan.

- What will you strive to do to help the district reach that identified goal?

- Who is your mentor? Describe what you're hoping to get from your mentee-mentor relationship. Hold yourself and your mentor accountable to ensure you get exactly what you need.

- Create a working list of education Twitter chats as well as days/times.

- Create a list of Education books you'd like to read over the course of the school year.

- Describe one way in which you hope to engage with peers this year.

- Describe one way in which you hope to engage your students in the learning process.

　

- Describe one way in which you hope to engage families and the community this year.

　

- What is one way that you're going to ensure your voice is heard?

- Write down a list of actionable goals to help bring about the eradication of any inequities (racial, gender, socioeconomic, etc.) you've seen in your school/district/state/country.

- Examine at least one piece of literature (novel/textbook/workbooks) through an equity lens. Whose voice is being heard? Whose voice is being silenced? Why? If it's not representative of the children you're serving, are there more appropriate sources that'll do so?

- Write down your ideas for the lesson you're most looking forward to getting started on with students. What are the desired outcomes? How will you ensure each student meets those outcomes?

_____
_____
_____
_____
_____
_____
_____
_____

- How do you plan on providing actionable feedback to students in a timely manner? What will your feedback loop look like?

_____
_____
_____
_____
_____
_____
_____
_____

- In terms of classroom management, write down your list of "non-negotiables."

_____
_____
_____
_____

- How will you ensure the amplification of student voice in your classroom?

- Finally, how will you go about demonstrating to students that your passion is to help them thrive both academically and socially? (It's easy to say it, but it takes work to prove it.)

OTHER EDUMATCH TITLES

EduMatch Snapshot in Education (2016)
In this collaborative project, twenty educators located throughout the United States share educational strategies that have worked well for them, both with students and in their professional practice.

The #EduMatch Teacher's Recipe Guide
Editors: Tammy Neil & Sarah Thomas
Dive in as fourteen international educators share their recipes for success, both literally and metaphorically!

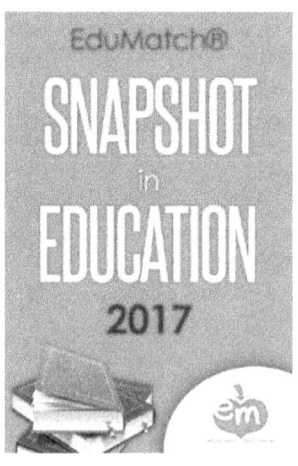

EduMatch Snapshot in Education (2017)
We're back! EduMatch proudly presents Snapshot in Education (2017). In this two-volume collection, 32 educators and one student share their tips for the classroom and professional practice.

OTHER EDUMATCH TITLES

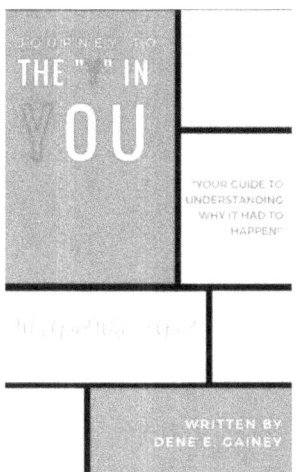

Journey to The "Y" in You by Dene Gainey
This book started as a series of separate writing pieces that were eventually woven together to form a fabric called The Y in You. The question is, "What's the 'why' in you?"

The Teacher's Journey by Brian Costello
Follow the Teacher's Journey with Brian as he weaves together the stories of seven incredible educators. Each step encourages educators at any level to reflect, grow, and connect.

OTHER EDUMATCH TITLES

The Fire Within
Compiled and edited by Mandy Froehlich
Adversity itself is not what defines us. It is how we react to that adversity and the choices we make that creates who we are and how we will persevere.

EduMagic by Sam Fecich
This book challenges the thought that "teaching" begins only after certification and college graduation. Instead, it describes how students in teacher preparation programs have value to offer their future colleagues, even as they are learning to be teachers!

OTHER EDUMATCH TITLES

Makers in Schools
Editors: Susan Brown & Barbara Liedahl
The maker mindset sets the stage for the Fourth Industrial Revolution, empowering educators to guide their students.

Divergent EDU by Mandy Froehlich
The concept of being innovative can be made to sound so simple. But what if the development of the innovative thinking isn't the only roadblock?

OTHER EDUMATCH TITLES

EduMatch Snapshot in Education (2018)
EduMatch® is back for our third annual Snapshot in Education. Dive in as 21 educators share a snapshot of what they learned, what they did, and how they grew in 2018.

Daddy's Favorites by Elissa Joy
Illustrated by Dionne Victoria
Five-year-old Jill wants to be the center of everyone's world. But, her most favorite person in the world, without fail, is her Daddy. But Daddy has to be Daddy, and most times that means he has to be there when everyone needs him, especially when her brother Danny needs him.

OTHER EDUMATCH TITLES

Level Up Leadership by Brian Kulak
Gaming has captivated its players for generations and cemented itself as a fundamental part of our culture. In order to reach the end of the game, they all need to level up.

DigCit Kids edited by Marialice Curran & Curran Dee
This book is a compilation of stories, starting with our own mother and son story, and shares examples from both parents and educators on how they embed digital citizenship at home and in the classroom.

OTHER EDUMATCH TITLES

Stories of EduInfluence by Brent Coley
In Stories of EduInfluence, veteran educator Brent Coley shares stories from more than two decades in the classroom and front office, stories illustrating the life-changing power we possess.

The Edupreneur by Dr. Will
The Edupreneur is a 2019 documentary film that takes you on a journey into the successes and challenges of some of the most recognized names in K-12 education consulting.

OTHER EDUMATCH TITLES

In Other Words by Rachelle Dene Poth
In Other Words is a book full of inspirational and thought-provoking quotes that have pushed the author's thinking, inspired her, and given her strength when she needed it.

To Whom it May Concern
Editors: Sarah-Jane Thomas, PhD & Nicol R. Howard, PhD
In *To Whom it May Concern...*, you will read a collaboration between two Master's in Education classes at two universities on opposite coasts

of the United States.

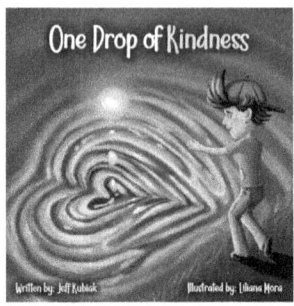

One Drop of Kindness by Jeff Kubiak
This children's book, along with each of you, will change our world as we know it. It only takes *One Drop of Kindness to fill a heart with love.*

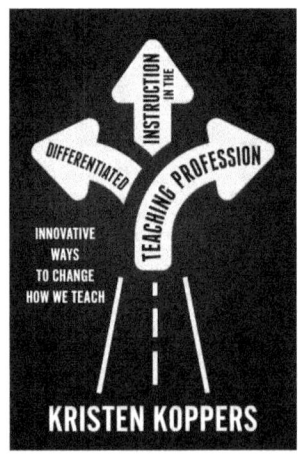

Differentiated Instruction in the Teaching Profession by Kristen Koppers
Differentiated Instruction in the Teaching Profession is an innovative way to use critical thinking skills to create strategies to help all students succeed. This book is for educators of all levels who want to take the next step into differentiating their instruction.

OTHER EDUMATCH TITLES

NOTES

5. GET TO KNOW YOUR PEERS

1. Collective Teacher Efficacy - *the belief of all teachers within a building that they can positively affect student achievement as a result of their professional ability and engagement in research and data analysis (Hattie).*

7. FAMILY ENGAGEMENT

1. https://www.youtube.com/channel/UC6QXBxa3Cn4ZME31BLWiVmA/featured?disable_polymer=1

9. AVOID THE PERPETUATION OF RACIAL INEQUITIES

1. *Note: parents were, of course, able to opt their child out of the book study. In that case, students would have been asked to read a book dealing with comparable thematic elements and plot structure.*

www.ingramcontent.com/pod-product-compliance
Lightning Source LLC
Chambersburg PA
CBHW071241070526
44583CB00017B/2284